CAVENDISH
LawCards®

G000079010

Cavendish
Publishing
Limited

London • Sydney

Second edition first published 1999 by Cavendish Publishing Limited, The Glass House, Wharton Street, London WC1X 9PX, United Kingdom

Telephone: +44 (0) 20 7278 8000

Facsimile: +44 (0) 20 7278 8080

E-mail: info@cavendishpublishing.com

Visit our Home Page on http://www.cavendishpublishing.com

British Library Cataloguing in Publication Data

Trusts – 2nd ed – (Cavendish law cards)

1. Trusts and trustees – England 2. Trusts and trustees – Wales

346.4'2'059

ISBN 1 85941 508 3

Printed and bound in Great Britain

Contents

1 The nature and types of trusts

A trust is a relationship which arises where one person (the trustee) is compelled in equity to hold property for the benefit of another (the beneficiary) or for a purpose permitted by law.

THE ANATOMY OF A TRUST

PROPERTY
(Anything capable of being owned)

↓

DUAL OWNERSHIP
(Resulting from equity's intervention)

↓

LEGAL OWNERSHIP
(Management/control)

EQUITABLE OWNERSHIP
(Beneficial enjoyment)

↓

TRUSTEE

BENEFICIARIES
(Individuals or private class)

PURPOSES
(Usually charitable)

Key elements of the trust

Property

Trusts are inextricably linked to property. As Lord Browne-Wilkinson emphasised in *Westdeutsche Landesbank Girozentrale v Islington LBC* (1996), 'in order to establish a trust, there must be identifiable trust property'. Anything that is capable of being owned may constitute trust property.

Equitable origin of the trust

From the outset, common law courts refused to recognise the rights of the beneficiary (B) against the trustee (T). By contrast, the Court of Chancery has always upheld these rights by imposing an equitable obligation on T.

Where a trust is for individuals or a private class of persons, this entitles them to enforce the trustee's obligations.

Where the trust is for a purpose which is beneficial to the public, it is enforceable by the Attorney General as a *charitable trust*. But, if the intended purpose is non-charitable, the trust can be enforced only in exceptional cases.

Duality of ownership

Under the common law, once trust property is vested in T, he is deemed to be the legal owner.

Equity does not dispute T's legal ownership but recognises B as the equitable owner of the trust property. In substance, this means that T is responsible for administering the trust property while B enjoys the benefits flowing from the property.

As Lord Browne-Wilkinson has pointed out in the *Westdeutsche* case, the most notable consequence of such equitable ownership is that, 'once a trust is established, as from that date of its establishment, the beneficiary has, in equity, *a proprietary interest* [italics mine] in the trust property'. The hallmarks of this interest are that:

- it is capable of being disposed of or acquired like any other interest in property;

- it may itself become the subject matter of a trust; for example, if T holds property on trust for B, B may declare himself a trustee of the interest for the benefit of Z;

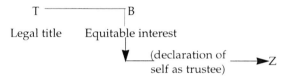

In the alternative, B may choose to transfer his interest to Y on trust for Z.

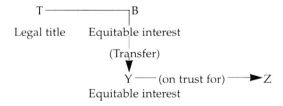

- it is enforceable not only *in personam* against the trustee but *in rem* against the whole world except a *bona fide purchaser for value without notice*. For example, if T wrongfully transfers trust property to A, B has a personal claim against T for mismanaging the trust while his interest in the property continues to subsist against A.

Classification of trusts

Public trusts and private trusts

Public Trusts		Private Trusts	
Type of trust/gift	Enforceability	Type of trust/gift	Enforceability
(1) Trust for specified charitable purpose	Enforceable by AG	(1) Trust for persons	Enforceable by beneficiaries
(2) Donations to charitable bodies	Enforceable by AG	(2) Trust for non-charitable purposes	Not ordinarily enforceable but may be upheld if for upkeep of tombs/pets and trustee is willing
		(3) Gift to unincorporated non-charitable body	Depends on whether it is construed as being on trust for its purposes or a gift to its members

Public or charitable trusts

A trust which promotes the well-being of the public by relieving poverty, advancing education, advancing religion or serving some other purpose beneficial to the community is enforceable by the Attorney General as a charitable trust.

Private trusts

A trust which is essentially for the benefit of individuals or a specified group of persons is enforceable by such beneficiaries as a private trust.

Difficulties arise where a trust is created not for the benefit of ascertainable persons but for a stated purpose which is not charitable. The general rule is that the trust will fail since there are no beneficiaries to enforce it. However, an exception is made in the case of trusts for the upkeep of pets or the maintenance of graves and tombs which have been held to be valid trusts of imperfect obligations: see, for example, *Re Dean* (1889) and *Re Hooper* (1932).

The problem of whether a trust/gift is for a purpose or for persons is particularly acute where property is given to an unincorporated association which does not have charitable purposes. Such a gift may be construed as giving rise to a trust for the association's purposes, in which case it is liable to fail as a non-charitable purpose trust. Alternatively, the gift may be construed as one to the members who collectively make up the association with the result that it will not fail for want of beneficiaries. As a rule, however, the individual members do not thereby acquire immediate distributive shares in the property given; rather it will be treated as an accretion to the association's assets to be applied for the benefit of the members. See *Leahy v AG (NSW)* (1959); *Neville Estates v Madden* (1962) and *Re Recher's WT* (1972).

Express trusts and trusts imposed on other grounds

Express trusts
An express trust arises as a result of a declaration of trust by a person in whom property is vested, for example, where:

- S, the owner of Blackacre, declares himself trustee of the property for B;

- S, the owner of Blackacre, conveys it to Z on trust for B (these are *inter vivos trusts* and S is a *settlor*);

- T leaves Blackacre in his will to Z with directions to hold it on trust for B (this is a *testamentary trust* and T is the *testator*);

Trusts imposed by equity on other grounds

There are numerous instances where equity will compel one party to hold property on trust for another even though a trust has not been formally declared. A trust imposed in such circumstances may be a *resulting* or *constructive* trust.

Resulting trusts

A resulting trust arises where B transfers or directs the transfer of property to which he is beneficially entitled to T in circumstances where equity deems it appropriate that T should hold the beneficial interest on trust for B. Such a trust may be a *presumed* resulting trusts or an *automatic* resulting trust: see *Re Vandervell's Trust (No 2)* (1974).

Constructive trusts

In general terms, the constructive trust is the residual category of trust. Such trusts have over the years been imposed in a wide variety of divergent situations in which the courts have found it necessary to compel a person to hold property for the benefit of another in the interests of justice and good conscience.

The following are examples of the types of situations in which the courts have been prepared to impose constructive trusts:

- where a fiduciary misappropriates property entrusted to him or has made unauthorised profits;

- where a third party knowingly receives trust property or is an accessory who dishonestly facilitates the trustee's breach of trust;

- where a statute enacted to prevent fraud is fraudulently used by one person to enrich himself at another's expense;

- where a person acquires legal title to property through killing another.

Statutory trusts

Even where there is no express declaration of trust, there are several contexts in which trusts have been imposed by statute, for example:

- under s 33 of the AEA 1925 as amended by the Trusts of Land and Appointment of Trustees Act (TLATA) 1996, which provides that, where a person dies intestate, his personal representatives shall hold his real and personal property on trust with a power to sell it;

- under the LPA 1925 (as amended by the TLATA), statutory trusts of land are imposed:

  › where a legal estate is beneficially limited to or held on trust for any persons as joint tenants (s 36);

  › where land is expressed to be conveyed to two or more persons in undivided shares. Such persons (or the first four if there are more than four) hold as joint tenants under a statutory trust (s 34);

- under s 27 of the SLA 1925 which has been superceded by the TLATA, an attempt to transfer a legal estate to an infant is effective as a declaration of trust of land by the person purporting to make the transfer.

Fixed, discretionary and protective trusts

Fixed trusts

It is open to a settlor or testator in creating a trust to specify the precise beneficial interest to be taken by each intended beneficiary. For example, S may give £10,000 to T:

- on trust for B1 for life remainder to B2; or

- on trust for B1 and B2 in equal shares.

Such trusts are described as fixed trusts.

Discretionary trusts

Alternatively, S may leave it to T to determine the manner in which trust capital, income or both should be distributed. Where S does so, a discretionary trust arises.

The discretionary trust is considered an appropriate way of holding property for two reasons:

- it allows account to be taken of alterations in circumstances of intended beneficiaries which may occur at a time when the settlor is no longer in a position to make required changes; and

- it provides a means of preventing the subject matter of the gift from being dissipated by a reckless beneficiary.

Protective trusts

The protective trust is known in certain jurisdictions as the *spendthrift trust.* It enables a balance to be struck between providing a beneficiary with a fixed share and encircling him with the safeguard of a discretionary trust.

The features of such a trust as outlined in s 33 of the TA 1925 are:

- that it confers a fixed interest on the intended beneficiary either for life or for a specified period of a lesser duration;

- that this interest shall determine before running its full course on the happening of certain events such as bankruptcy or attempted alienation; and

- that where the interest is determined a discretionary trust will arise in favour of the intended beneficiary and his wife and children.

Trusts and related concepts

In seeking to understand the nature of the trust, it is useful to compare it with various other concepts familiar to English law.

Trusts and bailment

Bailment entails delivery of goods for specified purposes after which the *bailee* must return them to the *bailor* or deliver them according to his directions.

Although a bailment is like a trust, to the extent that both entail the reliance by one person on another, there are differences:

BAILMENT	TRUST
Common law origin	Originated in equity
Subject matter = Goods	Subject matter = Any property
Passes special property (possession)	Transfers general property (ownership)
Bailee cannot pass good title unless statute permits (for example, Factors Act 1889)	Trustee passes good title to *bona fide* purchaser for value without notice

Trusts and contract

A contract is an agreement between parties which is intended to create legal relations. It differs from a trust in the following respects:

Contract	Trust
Enforceable both at law (damages) and in equity (specific performance; injunction, etc)	Enforceable only in equity
Obligations of contracting parties not always connected with property	Property-centred relationship
Enforcement only by parties to agreement	Enforcement not dependent on beneficiary's agreement
Consideration required except for agreements under seal	Not needed once trust property is vested in trustee

Note: The distinction between contracts and trusts is not always easy to discern where two persons make an agreement to confer a benefit on a third person; for example, A agrees with B to pay C £1,000. The traditional common law position has long been that C, not being a party to the agreement, cannot ordinarily enforce it in the realm of contract: see *Tweddle v Atkinson* (1861); *Dunlop v Selfridges* (1915); *Scruttons v Midland Silicones* (1962). Note, however, that the Contracts (Rights of Third Parties) Bill 1999 which is currently going through Parliament will confer on C a contractual right to enforce the agreement.

Notwithstanding the traditional common law position, the courts have established that, where A or B intended to contract as a trustee of the benefit for C, the importation of a trust into the contract between A and B makes it enforceable by C: see *Lloyds v Harper* (1880); *Les Affréteurs Réunis Société Anonyme v Leopold Walford* (1919); *Re Schebsman* (1944); *Don King Productions Inc v Warren* (1998); *Burton v FX Music* (1999).

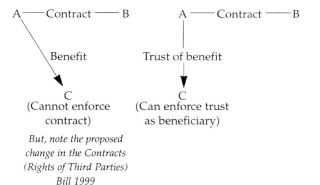

A —— Contract —— B	A —— Contract —— B
Benefit	Trust of benefit
C (Cannot enforce contract)	C (Can enforce trust as beneficiary)

But, note the proposed
change in the Contracts
(Rights of Third Parties)
Bill 1999

Trusts and agency

The main similarities between a trust and an agency are that:

- trustees like agents are *fiduciaries* who must act in utmost good faith; and
- trustees and agents are accountable for unauthorised profits.

Agency, however, differs from trusts in the following respects:

AGENCY	TRUST
Based on agreement between principal and agent	Agreement not a requirement
Primarily designed to bring principal into contractual relations with third party	Does not require any third party involvement
Essentially, a personal relationship not involving transfer of ownership (*Lister v Stubbs* (1890))	Gives rise to a proprietary relationship
Principal in same position as creditor on agent's insolvency	Beneficiary given priority over unsecured creditors in respect of trust property held by insolvent trustee

Trusts and powers

A power is an authority given by a donor to a donee to deal with or dispose of the donor's property: see *Freme v Clement* (1881).

The most notable type of power is the *power of appointment* under which the donee (or *appointor*) is authorised to appoint specified property to such persons (called objects or *appointees*) as the donee sees fit.

Trusts resemble powers insofar as both trustees and donees of powers are authorised to deal with or dispose of property belonging to the settlor or donor. There are, however, several significant differences between the two:

Powers	Trust
May be legal (for example, power of attorney) or equitable (for example, power of appointment)	Exclusively equitable
Discretionary in nature: (May be carried out)	Imperative/obligatory: (Must be carried out)
With particular reference to powers of appointment: • objects of power own nothing until power is exercised; • objects of power cannot absolutely entitled may compel donee to exercise power or transfer the property to them; • if appointment is not made there will be gift over in default or resulting trust	By contrast, in the case of trusts: • beneficiaries become owners once trust is constituted; • beneficiaries of full age/ demand trust property under rule in *Saunders v Vautier* (1841); • if trustee's duty to distribute is not carried out court will intervene to execute the trust

Over the years, however, the dividing line between trusts and powers has now become less clear cut as a result of the following developments:

- the modern trend towards conferring a wide range of powers and discretions on trustees by the trust instrument as well as by the various statutory provisions (including, most recently, ss 6–9 of the TLATA 1996).

  Powers which are conferred on trustees are called *fiduciary powers* and are distinguishable from *bare powers*, that is, those which are not held in a fiduciary capacity by the donee. In the case of a fiduciary power, the trustee is under a duty to consider from time to time whether to exercise it (see *Re May* (1982); whereas the donee of a bare power is under no such duty;

- the judicial recognition of the resemblance between powers of appointment and discretionary trusts in *McPhail v Doulton* (1971), a case which, according to Pearce and Stevens 'marks the major break from the traditional dichotomy between trusts and powers'. This resemblance prompted Lord Wilberforce to remark on the narrowness and artificiality of the distinction between trusts and powers and ultimately persuaded him to adopt the same test for certainty of objects for powers and discretionary trusts;

- the super imposition of trusts on arrangements which would otherwise be regarded as powers in cases like *Burrough v Philcox* (1840). This has resulted in the emergence of the *trust power* or *power in the nature of a trust*;

- the fundamental premise that trusts are imperative and powers discretionary has been eroded by:

- the willingness of the courts to give effect to *trusts of imperfect obligation* which have no human beneficiaries who may compel performance;

- the acceptance in cases like *Mettoy Pensions Trustees v Evans* (1990) that, where a fiduciary power conferred on a trustee is not exercised by him, the court may intervene and execute the power.

Spheres of application of the trust

According to Maitland, the trust is 'an institute of great elasticity and generality'. The truth of this assertion is borne out by the manner in which trusts have been employed in a wide variety of contexts. For instance:

- the affairs of infants, persons of unsound mind, bankrupt persons, etc, are commonly placed in the hands of competent trustees;

- the trust is frequently utilised as a device for preserving wealth within families (settlements, protective trusts, etc);

- recourse is often had to secret trusts by persons who wish to provide for others without attracting publicity;

- trusts have had a significant impact in the commercial sphere (for example, unit trusts and pension fund trusts);

- where an unincorporated association acquires property it is usual for such property to be held by trustees on its behalf;

- in the charitable domain, the trust serves as a vehicle for carrying out purposes beneficial to the community;

- finally, trusts are central to numerous complex and ingenious *tax saving schemes* which have become commonplace in recent years.

2 The creation of express trusts

The three certainties

In order for an express trust to be validly declared, three certainties must be present. These are:

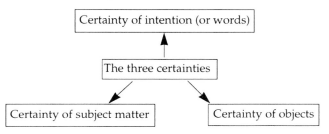

Certainty of intention (or words)

Imperative words required: In declaring a trust, the settlor must use imperative words to indicate that he intends to impose an obligation on the trustee. The easiest way of manifesting this intention is to include the word 'trust' or 'trustee' in the declaration, for example, 'To T on trust for B'. Even where the word 'trust' does not appear in the declaration, other imperative words (direct, require, instruct etc) will usually suffice, for example, S transfers Blackacre to T and states that 'I direct him to hold it for B': see *Re Le Cren Clarke* (1995).

In the absence of words which are clearly imperative, complications may arise at two levels:

- In some instances, it may be difficult to determine whether a *trust* or a *power* was intended. For example, £500,000 to X to be distributed among such of my nephews and nieces as X shall select:

- ○ if construed as a *trust* and X fails to select, the nephews and nieces will be entitled as a class;

- ○ if construed as a *power of appointment* and X fails to select, the money will revert to the donor or his estate.

- In other instances, the difficulty may lie in determining whether a *trust* or an *outright gift* was intended. This is especially the case where a gift of property is accompanied by *precatory words* as opposed to imperative words. For example, X transfers property to Y declaring that he wishes (or hopes/desires/suggests/believes) that Z will benefit from the property. Initially, the Chancellors took the view that gifts accompanied by precatory words imposed a trust on the donee: see, for example, *Harding v Glyn* (1739); *Hart v Tribe* (1854) and *Gully v Cregoe* (1857).

A new approach was signalled by *Lambe v Eames* (1871), which held that the use of precatory words in a gift did not mean that the donor intended the donee to hold the property on trust. This has been reinforced by other cases in which the courts have refused to enforce as trusts, gifts accompanied by precatory words. For example:

CASE	PRECATORY WORDS
Mussoorie Bank v Raynor (1882)	'Feeling confident'
Re Adams and Kensington Vestry (1884)	'In full confidence'
Re Diggles (1888)	'It is my desire'
Re Hamilton (1895)	'I wish them'
Re Williams (1897)	'In the fullest confidence'
Re Connolly (1910)	'I specifically desire'
Re Johnson (1945)	'I request that'

It is not, however, an absolute rule that a trust can never be created where precatory words are employed. On the contrary, if the instrument as a whole, or the context in which the precatory words are used, indicates that a trust was intended, the courts are quite prepared to give effect to the trust as seen from cases like *Re Hamilton; Comiskey v Bowring-Hanbury* (1905) and *Re Steele's WT* (1948).

Inferring intention to declare trust

The courts have sometimes discovered an intention to create a trust from the settlor's conduct where no trust was specifically declared. For example:

Case	Circumstances from which Trust was Inferred
Paul v Constence (1977) *Rowe v Prance* (1999)	Repeated assertions by A to B that A regarded property to which trust relates as belonging to B as much as it does to A
Re Kayford (1975)	Trading company's segregation of money paid by customers ordering goods from the rest of the company's funds
Dhingra v Dhingra (1999)	Bank account opened by father. Intention to create trust in son's favour inferred from the fact that bank statements recorded the account holder as being the father 'as trustee for' the son

Certainty of subject matter

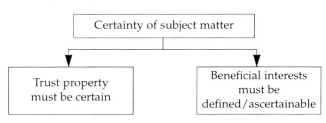

Certainty of subject matter

→ Trust property must be certain

→ Beneficial interests must be defined/ascertainable

Certainty as to the trust property

A trust is liable to fail unless the property covered by it is properly identified. Such failure may occur in the following contexts:

(a) *Where the property to be held on trust forms an undifferentiated part of a larger quantity:* This state of affairs is typified by *Re London Wine Co* (1975). LWC, the owner of a large stock of wine, declared that it would hold parts of its stock on trust for various buyers without taking any steps to set apart the respective quantities to be held on trusts from the bulk of its stock. The trust was declared invalid partly on the principle that this failure to segregate the wine to be held on trust rendered the subject matter of the trust uncertain. This meant that on LWC's insolvency the buyers had no priority over its other creditors. See, also, *Re Goldcorp* (1994).

In *Hunter v Moss* (1993), however, the Court of Appeal declined to apply the principle in *Re London Wine Co* in circumstances where M, who owned 950 shares in a company, declared himself a trustee of 50 shares for H without specifying the shares. The trust was upheld as valid on the basis that the shares were intangible assets of identical value and so specific appropriation was not needed to make the subject matter of the trust certain. This has subsequently been endorsed in *Re Harvard Securities Ltd* (1997).

It is also noteworthy that, in the specific context of sale of goods transactions, the effect of *Re London Wine Co* has now largely been reversed by the Sale of Goods (Amendment) Act 1995. Under this Act, buyers of unsegregated consignments of goods forming part of a larger bulk are now collectively regarded as tenants in common of the legal title to the bulk and, as such, will have priority over the seller's other creditors in respect of such goods.

(b) *Where relative words are employed in defining the property:*
Failure of a trust on this account is exemplified by *Palmer v Simmonds* (1854) which involved a gift by a testatrix of 'the bulk' of her residuary estate and *Re Kolb* (1962) which concerned a direction to hold 'blue chip securities' on trust.

Note, however, the more flexible approach in *Re Golay's WT* (1965) with regard to a trust to pay a reasonable income to a named beneficiary.

(c) *Where property is given to one person subject to a gift of an unspecified part of the property to some other person:* A gift of this nature was held to be uncertain in *Sprange v Barnard* (1789), where T left a sum of money for H directing that at H's death any part of this sum which he did not require was to go to X,Y and Z equally: see also *Curtis v Rippon* (1820).

A more accommodating approach is, however, evident in the context of *mutual wills* and *secret trusts.* These sometimes involve testamentary gifts of property to a person who is supposed to leave whatever part of it he has not utilised for himself in his lifetime to some other person. As seen from cases such as *Birmingham v Renfrew* (1937) and *Re Cleaver* (1981) (mutual wills) and *Ottaway v Norman* (1972) (secret trust), the courts have endorsed such arrangements (which they characterise as 'floating trusts') despite the inherent uncertainty regarding their subject matter.

Certainty as to beneficial interests

A trust in favour of more than one beneficiary may fail because it is impossible to ascertain the interests to be taken by the beneficiaries. In *Boyce v Boyce* (1849), for instance, T left two houses to trustees who were to convey to his daughter M whichever one she chose and to hold the one not chosen by M on trust for his other daughter C. M died before choosing and the trust in C's favour failed because her interest was uncertain.

A trust will not, however, fail on this account where a settlor or testator creates a discretionary trust under which the trustees are to determine the interests of the various beneficiaries; or where the court discovers a workable formula for distribution as in *Re Knapton* (1941), where lots were used to determine the entitlement of beneficiaries.

Certainty of objects
The objects of charitable trusts are the purposes for which they are created; while the objects of non-charitable (private) trusts are the intended beneficiaries. A non-charitable trust is effective only if these beneficiaries are ascertained or ascertainable.

Where there are no identifiable beneficiaries (for example, because the trust is essentially for a purpose), the trust will fail as there will be no one to enforce it: see *Re Hummeltenberg* (1923); *Re Endacott* (1960) and *Re Astor's ST* (1952).

Certainty of objects in the context of trusts for individuals
The requirement of certainty is easily fulfilled in the case of trusts for the benefit of named individuals, for example, '£10,000 to T on trust for Bill Bloggs'.

Where individual beneficiaries are not named but identified by description, the requirement is satisfied once an individual who fits the description can be identified, for example, '£1,000 to T on trust for the oldest person living on the Bleak Estate, Swansea'.

Trusts for a class of persons

Where a trust is not for specified individuals, but for a designated class, it can only be carried out if there is sufficient certainty to enable the trustees to tell who belongs to the class.

Where class gifts are concerned, uncertainty may be present:

- because the language used to describe the class is open to different interpretations (conceptual uncertainty); or

- because the evidence needed to establish who belongs to the class is incomplete (evidential uncertainty).

In determining whether there is certainty of objects, the courts have distinguished between *fixed trusts* and *discretionary trusts*.

Fixed trusts

A fixed trust arises, for instance, where S transfers £100,000 to T on trust for S's brothers in equal shares. In this type of trust, S's directions can only be carried out where the size of the class and identities of all the members are known to or capable of ascertainment by T.

The test for deciding whether the objects of such a trust are certain is to consider whether a *comprehensive list* can be made, which accurately includes the names of all those who are beneficially entitled, while excluding all those who fall outside the class: see *IRC v Broadway Cottages* (1955); *Re Gulbenkian's ST* (1970) and *McPhail v Doulton* (1971).

If a comprehensive list cannot be drawn up because the description of the class is conceptually uncertain, the trust will fail, for example, '£10,000 on trust for all my old friends in equal shares': see *Re Gulbenkian's ST* (1970) and *Brown v Gould* (1972). Even where the class is described in terms which are conceptually certain, the trust will still fail if it is impossible to draw up such a list because there is evidential uncertainty.

Discretionary trusts

A settlor who declares a trust in favour of a class may opt not to fix the shares of individual members and give the trustee a discretion to determine these shares. Before 1970, the test for certainty for discretionary trusts was the comprehensive list test applicable to fixed trusts: see *Re Ogden* (1933); *IRC v Broadway Cottages* (1955) and *Re Sayer* (1957).

The comprehensive list test was, however, discarded by the House of Lords in the landmark case of *McPhail v Doulton* which concerned a discretionary trust in favour of a certain Mr Baden's 'employees', 'ex-employees', their 'relatives' and 'dependants'. Their Lordships preferred the less stringent test formulated for powers in *Re Gestetner* (1953) and *Re Gulbenkian*. Under this test, the decisive criterion is whether the words employed in describing the discretionary class are such that it can be said with certainty that any individual *is or is not* a member of that class.

The *Baden* saga did not end in the House of Lords since the case was remitted to the High Court, and thence to the Court of Appeal (under the name *Re Baden (No 2)*) to determine whether the reference to 'relatives' and 'dependants' rendered the trust uncertain. In determining this issue, all three Court of Appeal judges embraced the 'is-is not' test but each judge approached the test from a different perspective. *Stamp LJ* adopted a strict literal approach, arguing that for the test to be satisfied the trustee had to be able to say of *any* individual that he either is or is not within the class.

The test was construed less rigidly by *Megaw LJ* and *Sachs LJ*. The former signified that the test would be satisfied if, as regards a substantial number of objects, it could be said with certainty that they fell within the class even though, as regards a substantial number of others, it could not be proven whether they are within or outside the class. For his part, the latter maintained that whether a person fell within the class or not was a question of fact and, if a given claimant could not prove that he was within the class then he could be taken to be outside it.

Curing uncertainty by reference to opinions of third parties

Where a trust would ordinarily fail, because the class of beneficiaries is defined in conceptually uncertain terms, will such a trust be rendered valid by the provision in the trust instrument of some mechanism for the trustee or a third party to determine the meaning to be ascribed to such terms?

Academic opinion is divided on this matter. Martin asserts that:

> ... conceptual uncertainty may in some cases be cured by providing that the opinion of a third party ... is to settle the matter.

By contrast, others like Hayton and Riddall maintain that conceptual uncertainty cannot be resolved by such provisions. According to Hayton:

> If the concept is my tall relations or my old friends or my good business associates and the trustees are given the power to resolve any doubt as to whether a person qualifies or not, ... since ... the court cannot resolve this conceptual uncertainty it is difficult to see how the trustees can.

There is a similar divergence of judicial opinion. In *Re Tuck's ST* (1978), Lord Denning saw no reason why a trust instrument should not provide that any dispute or doubt should be resolved by the trustees or others. See, also, *Re Leek* (1969). This view does not appear to be shared by Jenkins J, who stated in *Re Coxen* (1948) that a gift will not be saved by making provision for reference to be made to the opinion of trustees where the testator (or settlor) has himself insufficiently defined the state of affairs on which the trustees are to form their opinion.

Trusts with a power of selection

As seen from *Burrough v Philcox* (1840) (in Chapter 1), a trust may sometimes be super-imposed on a power of appointment, for example, if X empowers Y to distribute £100,000 among his nephews and nieces as he sees fit and directs that in default of distribution they are to take the £100,000 in equal shares. Where this happens, it appears that the test for powers/discretionary trusts will at the outset determine whether the class is sufficiently certain. If, in due course, Y defaults in making the selection, a fixed trust arises and the stricter test laid down in *IRC v Broadway Cottages* comes into play.

Gifts expressed to be subject to a condition precedent

Fixed trusts in favour of a class differ materially from trusts which confer a series of separate gifts on individuals who fulfil a condition or fall within a description, for example:

- if T is given £500,000 on trust to divide it equally among the settlor's old friends, this is a fixed trust in favour of a class which will fail for uncertainty of objects under the comprehensive list test. By contrast:

- if T is given £500,000 and directed to pay £1,000 to each of the settlor's old friends, this gives rise to a series of individual gifts in favour of persons falling within this description. As seen from *Re Barlow's WT* (1979), the comprehensive list test does not apply to this type of trust.

  The applicable test as laid down in *Re Allen* (1953) is that such a trust will not fail for uncertainty of objects once it is possible to say of at least one person that he or she satisfies the description of an old friend.

The criteria for determining whether the objects of a trust are sufficiently certain may be summarised in the diagram opposite.

Formalities for creation of express trusts

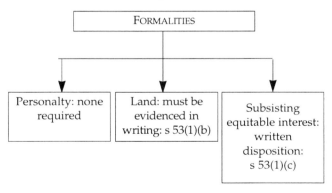

A person who wishes to create an express trust must ensure that he observes any formal requirements imposed by statute. There are different requirements for *inter vivos* and testamentary trusts.

*Criteria for determining whether the objects of a trust are
sufficiently certain*

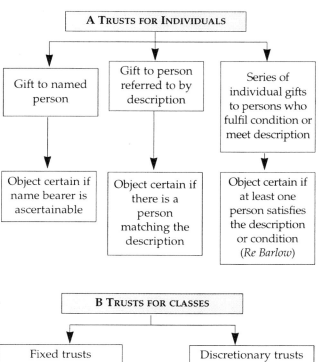

A TRUSTS FOR INDIVIDUALS

Gift to named person → Object certain if name bearer is ascertainable

Gift to person referred to by description → Object certain if there is a person matching the description

Series of individual gifts to persons who fulfil condition or meet description → Object certain if at least one person satisfies the description or condition (*Re Barlow*)

B TRUSTS FOR CLASSES

Fixed trusts → Objects certain if comprehensive list test is satisfied (*IRC v Broadway Cottages*)

Discretionary trusts → Objects certain if 'is/is not' test is satisfied (*McPhail v Doulton; Re Baden's DT*)

Inter vivos trusts

Trusts of personalty

Where the owner of personal property sets out to declare a trust of such property, he is not obliged to comply with any formal requirements. The effect of this, as pointed out by Dillon J in *Hunter v Moss,* is that 'it is well known that a trust of personalty can be created orally'.

But, note, that different considerations apply where the person creating a trust of personalty is the equitable owner of the property while legal ownership resides elsewhere (see below, pp 29–30).

Trusts of land

Where the subject matter of a trust is land, writing has been an important requirement since the enactment of the Statute of Frauds 1677. It has long been the case that a purchaser of land which is held on trust must pay the purchase price to at least two trustees. The use of writing, where a trust relates to land, reduces the likelihood of inadvertent non-compliance by a purchaser with the 'two trustee' rule.

The requirement of writing is now embodied in s 53(1)(b) of the LPA 1925 which provides that a declaration of trust respecting land or an interest in land must be manifested and proved by some writing signed by some person able to declare the trust. See, for example, *Bristol and West BS v Pritchard* (1994).

The following points should be noted with regard to s 53(1)(b):

- the actual declaration need not be in writing. A document acknowledging a prior oral declaration will suffice as seen from *Forster v Hale* (1798); *Childers v Childers* (1857) and *McBlain v Cross* (1871);

- the document must show that a trust was intended but need not contain all its terms : see *Re Tyler's Fund Trust* (1967);

- the document must be signed by the person able to declare the trust (that is, the owner of the land or interest which is the subject matter of the trust). An agent's signature will not suffice: see *Re Northcliffe* (1925);

- the requirement of writing was introduced to prevent fraud and the courts will not allow it to be used as a cloak for fraud as seen from cases like *Rochefoucauld v Bousted* (1897); *Bannister v Bannister* (1948) and *Hodgson v Marks* (1971).

Subsisting equitable interests

The owner of an equitable interest in property may confer the benefit of the interest on another person by: (i) assigning the interest to the donee; (ii) assigning it to a trustee for the donee; or (iii) declaring himself a trustee for the donee.

Section 53(1)(c) of the LPA provides that a *disposition* of an equitable interest or trust *subsisting* at the time of the disposition must be in writing, signed by the person disposing of the same or by his agent thereunto lawfully authorised in writing.

The following points should be noted with regard to s 53(1)(c):

- under s 53(1)(c), the disposition must be in writing. Evidence in writing of a prior oral disposition will not suffice;

- the document disposing of the equitable interest need not be signed by the owner. It may be signed by his agent;

- s 53(1)(c) applies not only to equitable interests in land (see *Ivin v Blake* (1993)) but also to equitable interests in personalty: see *Grey v IRC* (1960) and *Vandervell v IRC* (1967);

- the use of the word *subsisting* is significant. It means that where the owner of a legal estate or interest in property declares a trust this will not be governed by s 53(1)(c) since this involves creating a new equitable interest rather than disposing of a subsisting equitable interest.

Example 1: If S pays £10,000 into T1's bank account, orally declaring at the time that T1 should hold this money on trust for B1, this is valid. But, if B1 then orally declares that his interest in the £10,000 is to be held by T2 on trust for B2, this is invalid under s 53(1)(c).

Example 2: If S, the freehold owner of Blackacre, orally declares that he will hold it on trust for B, s 53(1)(c) will not apply. However, under s 53(1)(b), there must be some evidence in writing in support of this oral declaration.

Dispositions which fall within the ambit of s 53(1)(c)

The owner of an equitable interest may enter into a variety of transactions and arrangements involving his interest. The courts have been called upon from time to time to determine which of these transactions and arrangements qualify as dispositions within the meaning of s 53(1)(c). The position in this regard may be summarised as follows:

Type of Transaction/ Arrangement	Is it a Disposition which must be in writing under s 53(1)(c)?
Assignment of subsisting equitable interest to trustee	Yes
Direction to trustee with legal title to hold subsisting equitable interest on trust for third party	Yes: *Grey v IRC*
Direction to trustee with legal title to transfer property to third party	Need not comply with s 53(1)(c): see *Vandervell v IRC*.
Declaration of new trust by resulting trustee with consent of equitable owner	Upheld in *Re Vandervell (No 2)* despite non-compliance with s 53(1)(c)
Specifically enforceable contract to assign subsisting equitable interest	Not clearly settled in *Oughtred v IRC* whether such contract is a disposition which must be in writing. However, minority view of Lord Radcliffe that such a contract passes an equitable interest under a constructive trust even if oral has been endorsed by CA in *Neville v Wilson*
Declaration by owner of subsisting equitable interest of himself as trustee	Passive trust regarded as disposition under s 53(1)(c) but not active trust
Disclaimer of beneficial interest	Not a disposition under s 53(1)(c) according to *Re Paradise Motor Co; Allied Dunbar v Fowler*
Nomination of death benefits under pension scheme or life insurance policy	Not a disposition under s 53(1)(c) according to *Re Danish Bacon Co; Gold v Hill*

(1) *Assignment of equitable interest to trustee:* Where O, the owner of an equitable interest, assigns his interest to T on trust for B, this is undoubtedly a disposition within the meaning of s 53(1)(c) and will be void if it is not in writing.

(2) *Direction to trustee to hold on trust for another party:* Where O, the equitable owner of property held on trust by T as his nominee, directs T to hold the property on trust for B, *Grey v IRC* establishes that this is a disposition which must be in writing.

(3) *Transfer of legal title by trustee on direction of equitable owner:* Where O, the equitable owner of property held on trust by T, directs T to transfer the property outright to B, *Vandervell v IRC* has held that s 53(1)(c) will not apply. Thus, once T passes the legal title to B, there is no need for O to divest himself of his equitable interest by means of a written disposition.

(4) *Declaration of new trust by trustee with consent of equitable owner:* If T, who holds property on a resulting trust for O, declares a trust of the property for B's benefit with O's knowledge and consent, it appears from *Re Vandervell's Trusts (No 2)* (1974) that this is not a disposition under s 53(1)(c).

(5) *Oral contract to assign a subsisting equitable interest:* Where O owns an equitable interest which he orally agrees to assign to B for valuable consideration, judicial opinions are divided on whether s 53(1)(c) is applicable. Such an arrangement arose in *Oughtred v IRC* (1960), where it was argued that a specifically enforceable oral contract by the owner of an equitable interest in shares to transfer these shares conferred an equitable interest on the transferee without any need to comply with s 53(1)(c). While this argument did not prevail in the House of Lords in this case, the reasoning behind it has since been accepted in other contexts in *Re Holt's Settlement* (1969); *DHN Food Distributors v Tower Hamlets LBC* (1976); *Chinn v Collins* (1981); and *Neville v Wilson* (1996).

(6) *Declaration of self as trustee:* It is not conclusively settled whether s 53(1)(c) applies where O, who owns an equitable interest in property held on trust by T, declares himself a trustee of his interest for B. On the one hand, *Grainge v Wilberforce* (1889) and the judgment of Upjohn J in *Grey v IRC* (1960) signify that such a declaration with nothing more places B in a position to require T to convey the property according to his directions while O drops out of the picture. It appears, in effect, that such an arrangement is a disposition under s 53(1)(c) and not merely a declaration.

On the other hand, where O in declaring the trust retains active responsibilities as trustee so that he does not drop out of the picture, it appears that this is more akin to a declaration that a disposition as contemplated by s 53(1)(c): see *Re Lashmar* (1891).

(7) *Disclaimer of beneficial interest*: It emerges from cases such as *Re Paradise Motor Co* (1968) and *Allied Dunbar v Fowler* (1994) that, where a person who would otherwise be entitled to an equitable interest disclaims his interest, this will not be caught by s 53(1)(c) since disclaimer operates by way of avoidance and not by way of disposition.

(8) *Nomination of death benefits*: Where a member of an occupational pension scheme or the holder of a life insurance policy nominates a person who will receive benefits in the event of his death, this does not operate as a disposition under s 53(1)(c) as seen from cases such as *Re Danish Bacon Co* (1971) and *Gold v Hill* (1998).

Exemption of resulting and constructive trusts from statutory formalities

In a variety of situations where arrangements pertaining to property are subject to statutory formalities, such formalities are dispensed with if the circumstances point to the existence of a resulting or constructive trust. This was the case, for instance, in the recent case of *Yaxley v Gotts* (1999) which involved an oral 'gentleman's agreement' between Y and G, whereby Y was to undertake extensive renovation work on all the flats in a building owned by G and would, in return, be given two ground floor flats. G sought to resist Y's claim to these flats, contending that their agreement was not in writing as dictated by s 2 of the Law of Property (Miscellaneous Provisions) Act 1989. The Court of Appeal, however, upheld Y's claim on the ground that the agreement gave rise to a constructive trust.

In line with the foregoing, s 53(2) of the LPA states that the formal requirements prescribed in s 53(1)(b) and 53(1)(c) do not apply to the creation of resulting, implied or constructive trusts. The effect of this exclusion is evident in cases like *Bannister v Bannister* (1948) and *Neville v Wilson* (1996).

In *Bannister*, X agreed to sell her cottage to Y for less than its value and in return Y orally declared that he would allow X to live in the cottage rent free. It was held that Y held the cottage on constructive trust for X even though there was no evidence in writing as required by s 53(1)(b).

In *Neville*, the shareholders of a family company agreed to dissolve it and distribute the shares among themselves in the proportion of their shareholding. The Court of Appeal held that the agreement constituted each shareholder an implied trustee of the shares for the other shareholders and was not required to be in writing as required by s 53(1)(c).

Secret trusts

Statutory formalities for testamentary gifts

A person who wishes to create a trust that will take effect on his death is required by s 9 of the Wills Act 1837 to execute a formal will.

Secret trusts and the formalities requirement

A secret trust typically comes into being where a testator (T) leaves property in his will to a devisee (D) or a legatee (L) and instructs D or L to hold the property on trust for the benefit of a beneficiary (B) who is not mentioned in the will. Unlike the common law which does not recognise B's interest once it was not embodied in the will, equity is able to give effect to T's intention by enforcing the trust against D or L. There are two types of secret trusts, namely:

FULLY SECRET TRUST (FST)	HALF SECRET TRUST (HST)
Where the existence of a trust is not manifest in the will, for example, T's will gives £5,000 to L but before executing it T tells L to hold the sum on trust for B	Where trust is declared in the will without disclosing objects, for example, T leaves Blackacre to D on trust for persons communicated to D before executing the will

Note: Where T states in his will that L is to apply the property in a manner communicated elsewhere, but uses precatory language in the will, there will not be a HST. A FST may, however, arise if the communication outside the will is expressed in imperative terms: see *Re Spencer's Will* (1887).

Conditions for the enforcement of the FST:

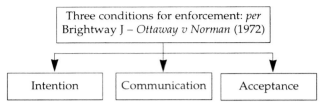

Three conditions for enforcement: *per* Brightway J – *Ottaway v Norman* (1972)

| Intention | Communication | Acceptance |

(a) *Intention*: T must manifest an intention to impose a binding obligation on L to hold the property left to him on trust for B. If T's words suggest that it is open to L to decide whether or not to apply the property for B's benefit, there will be no FST: see *McCormick v Grogan* (1869); *Re Snowden* (1979) and *Kasperbauer v Griffith* (1997).

(b) *Communication*: T must in his lifetime communicate his intention to L either before or after the will is executed. If not, L can claim the property beneficially: see *Wallgrave v Tebbs* (1855).

Where T conveys his intention to create the trust to L but does not in his lifetime communicate its terms and a letter containing the terms emerges after T's death, *Re Boyes* (1884) has decided that the FST will fail. But note that, if T gives L a sealed letter containing the terms not to be opened by L until T's death, this is *constructive communication* and the FST will not fail.

(c) *Acceptance*: L will be bound by the FST only if he has accepted to carry it out. Acceptance is usually express, but the courts may also imply acceptance on the basis of tacit acquiescence, where T's intention has been communicated to L who remains silent: see *Moss v Cooper* (1861) and *Ottaway v Norman* (1972).

Where there is no acceptance because T's intention was not communicated, L can take the property beneficially: see *Wallgrave v Tebbs*.

The position is less certain where communication is made to L who refuses the trust but T nevertheless leaves the property to him. It is not entirely clear whether, in such an event, L is bound to hold the property on a resulting trust for T's estate or becomes beneficially entitled to the property.

Once L accepts the terms communicated by T, any additions to the objects or subject matter proposed by T will be enforceable only if duly communicated and accepted: see *Re Colin Cooper* (1939).

Acceptance where there are two or more legatees/devisees
Where T in his will leaves property to L1 and L2 intending that they should hold it as co-trustees for B, problems will arise if the trust is communicated to and accepted by L1 but not L2. The applicable principles are to be found in *Re Stead* (1900).

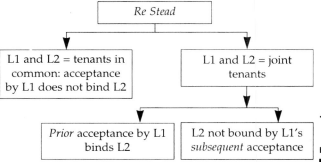

According to *Re Stead*, the position depends on whether the property has been left to them as joint tenants or tenants in common.

Where the property is left to L1 and L2 as tenants in common (for example, 'To L1 and L2 in equal shares'), each of them is deemed to have a separate and distinct interest in the property. Accordingly, where L1 alone accepts the trust, L2 will not be bound by it.

Where L1 and L2 are joint tenants (for example, 'To L1 and L2 jointly' or 'To L1 and L2') and L1 alone accepts the trust before the will is executed this will bind L2. By contrast, if L1 accepts after execution, L2 will not be bound by this.

Conditions for the enforcement of the HST

The HST was judicially recognised only comparatively recently in the leading case of *Blackwell v Blackwell* (1929). A HST, like a FST, is enforceable only where intention, communication and acceptance are present.

(a) *Intention*: A HST can only arise where T's intention to impose a trust is declared with sufficient certainty in the will itself.

(b) *Communication*: A HST which is not effectively communicated to the intended trustee will fail. The issue of communication was addressed in *Re Keen* (1937), which laid down two fundamental principles, as follows:

(1) the manner of communicating the objects/purposes to the intended trustee which is specified in the will must be consistent with the manner in which such communication actually occurs; and

(2) in any event, communication of the objects/purposes of the trust must occur before or at the time the will is executed. See, also, *Blackwell v Blackwell* and *Re Bateman's WT* (1970). Note that commentators like Holdsworth, Sheridan and Mee have heavily criticised this prior communication rule. In the judicial sphere, Carnwath J has also expressed reservations about the prior communication rule in *Gold v Hill*, where he referred approvingly to the suggestion in *Snell's Principles of Equity* that, 'in principle, there seems to be no real reason why the communication of the trust at any time before the testator's death should not suffice for the half secret as well as the fully secret trust'.

(c) *Acceptance*: A HST is liable to fail if the intended trustee does not accept that he will hold the property on trust for the beneficiary. This does not, however, entitle the trustee to take the property beneficially since he is obliged to hold it on a resulting trust for the testator's estate.

Re Stead decided that acceptance by one of two joint tenants before the execution of the will makes a FST enforceable against the other. The courts are yet to pronounce on the position where the same situation occurs in the context of a HST. It may, however, be inferred from *Re Stead* that the HST will be enforceable against the trustee who did not accept since (i) it is usual for trustees under a HST to hold as joint tenants; and (ii) communication of the trust must be before the will is executed.

Position where intended trustee predeceases testator or disclaims the gift

In the case of a HST, the death of the trustee in the testator's lifetime or his renunciation of the trust will not invalidate the trust even if he was the sole trustee named in the will.

The equitable maxim that a trust will not fail for want of trustees applies with full rigour in such cases.

The position is less clear cut where a FST is involved. On the one hand, Cozens-Hardy indicated in *Re Maddock* (1902) that such a trust will fail if the legatee/devisee dies in the testator's lifetime or disclaims the gift. This may be contrasted with *Re Blackwell* (1925), where Lord Buckmaster took the view that, where the evidence pointed to a FST, such a disclaimer or renunciation would not cause the trust to fail (although he did not comment on the effect of the intended trustee dying before the testator).

The basis for the enforcement of secret trusts

(a) *The fraud theory:* The traditional justification adopted by the courts for enforcing secret trusts is the prevention of fraud. See the judgment of Lord Westbury in *McCormick v Grogan* and Lord Sumner in *Blackwell v Blackwell*.

One variant of the fraud theory is that, unless the trust is upheld, the legatee/devisee will take the property beneficially, thereby unjustly enriching himself. This is not entirely convincing on two grounds:

(a) it is arguable that unjust enrichment can equally be prevented by means of a resulting trust for the testator's estate; and

(b) preventing unjust enrichment is immaterial in the case of a half secret trust which by its nature does not allow a trustee to take beneficially.

Another variant of this theory is that the fraud stems not from possible unjust enrichment but from the fact that, unless the trust is upheld, the testator's wishes will be thwarted and the beneficiaries will forego their entitlements: see, for example, *Riordan v Banon* (1876); *Re Fleetwood* (1880) and *Blackwell v Blackwell*. This explanation has found favour with some commentators (for example, Hodge [1980] Conv 341) but has been called into question by others (for example, Oakley, *Constructive Trusts*, p 118).

(b) *The 'dehors' theory:* An alternative explanation for enforcing secret trusts is now widely accepted in judicial and academic circles. This is that they are not in fact created in the will but arise *dehors* (that is, outside and independent of) the will.

This presupposes that the trust is declared *inter vivos* when the relevant communication and acceptance occur and thus it need not comply with the formalities in s 9 of the Wills Act. The function of the will is to *vest* the property in the trustee thereby enabling the beneficiary to enforce the trust against him. Two cases vividly illustrate operation of the *dehors* theory:

- *Re Young* (1951): which held that s 15 of the Wills Act which prevents a witness to a will from taking a benefit under it did not deprive a beneficiary under a secret trust of his entitlement on account of having witnessed the will; and

- *Re Gardner (No 2)* (1993): which held that the interest of a beneficiary under a secret trust did not lapse where the beneficiary had died before the testatrix, as it would have done if the trust had arisen under the will rather than outside it.

Are secret trusts express trusts or constructive trusts?

This is an issue which has generated considerable debate:

- Writers like Pettitt and Oakley favour the view that they should be treated as express trusts.

- By contrast, judges like Brightman J in *Ottaway v Norman* (1972); Nourse J in *Re Cleaver* (1981) and Moritt J in *Re*

Dale (1993) refer to them as constructive trusts and this is echoed by Hodge.

- Other commentators like Sheridan and Hayton and Marshall suggest that HSTs are undoubtedly express trusts, whereas FSTs which have been traditionally associated with the fraud theory can properly be regarded as constructive trusts.

The express-constructive trust debate is especially relevant where a secret trust relates to land because under s 53(1)(b) communication of the trust must be evidenced in writing if it is express but not if it is constructive.

The position has not yet been judicially resolved but note:

- *Re Baillie* (1886): HST unenforceable in the absence of writing.

- *Ottaway v Norman* (1972): FST based on oral declaration upheld without regard to the possibility that s 53(1)(b) might render it unenforceable. See, also, *Brown v Porau* (1995).

The constitution of trusts

Once an intention to make an outright gift or create a trust is declared, it must be determined whether the gift or trust is completely constituted. It is completely constituted when the property becomes vested in the donee or trustee. Where there has been a declaration but no vesting, the gift or trust is incompletely constituted.

The significance of vesting

- Where vesting has occurred, the donor/settlor can no longer change his mind and reclaim the property: see *Re Bowden* (1936).

- In addition, the donee/beneficiary obtains an enforceable interest in the property even if he gave no consideration. See, for example, *Jeffreys v Jeffreys* (1841) and *Paul v Paul* (1882).

- Where there has been no vesting, unless a donee/beneficiary has furnished consideration, he has no basis in equity for enforcing the trust against the donor/trustee. This is reflected in the general rule that *equity will not assist a volunteer to perfect an imperfect gift*: see *Milroy v Lord* (1862). A recent illustration of the type of situation in which the rule may come into effect was given by Lord Goff in *White v Jones* (1995), namely, where an *inter vivos* gift fails because the instrument transferring the property is defective. If the donor has, in the meantime, changed his mind, the donee cannot compel him to execute a new instrument since equity will not perfect an imperfect gift.

Constitution where settlor declares himself a trustee

Where a person declares himself a trustee of his own property for the benefit of another, the trust will be completely constituted when the declaration is made since the property will already be vested in the settlor. This is so even if the intended beneficiary is unaware of the declaration: see *Middleton v Pollock* (1876); *Standing v Bowring* (1885).

The following points should be noted with regard to self-constitution:

- Where the subject matter of the trust is land, s 53(1)(b) of the LPA requires the declaration to be in writing or evidenced in writing.

- Writing is also required where the person declaring himself a trustee owns only an equitable interest in the property concerned if this qualifies as a disposition under s 53(1)(c).

- Where a trust is declared with some other person as the trustee but vesting has not occurred, the beneficiary cannot seek to enforce the trust by claiming that the settlor declared himself a trustee: see *Milroy v Lord*. By the same token, if a donor sets out to make an outright gift but does not vest the property in the donee, the gift will not be enforced on the basis that the donor declared himself a trustee: see *Jones v Lock* (1865); *Richards v Delbridge* (1874) and *Hemmens v Wilson Browne* (1993).

Constitution where settlor is not the trustee

Where a settlor opts to create a trust with someone else as trustee (or an outright gift is made) it is completely constituted when the property is transferred to the trustee (or donee). The law lays down different modes of transfer for various types of property – see the diagram opposite.

Exceptional situations where vesting is deemed to have occurred in equity

(a) *Where the donor/settlor has made every effort:* At common law, property does not vest unless the formalities governing transfer are satisfied in the minutest detail. Equity, however, recognises that vesting takes place once a donor/settlor has done everything in his power to divest himself of the property even if the law requires some further task (such as registration) to be performed by a third party: see *Re Rose* (1952) and *Mascall v Mascall* (1985) but contrast with *Re Fry* (1946).

(b) *Where vesting occurs by other means:* This has three dimensions:

(1) Where a donor expresses an intention to make an immediate gift of property but dies not having transferred it to the donee, the gift will ordinarily founder on the principle that equity will not assist the donee to perfect the gift. The donee may, however, be in a position to claim the property if he is able to rely on the rule in *Strong v Bird* (1874). As explained in *Collier v Calvert* (1994), the effect of this rule is that:

> ... where the donor maintains an intention to make a gift but does not perfect it and dies having appointed the donee personal representative of the estate so that legal title vests on the death of the donor in the donee, [equity's] assistance is no longer required to order the transfer of the legal title to the donee ... In view of the continuing wishes of the donor in such circumstances, no one has a better equity than the donee. So equity refuses to intervene against the donee.

(2) Where S declares his intention to transfer property to T to hold on trust for B and the property becomes vested in T in a different capacity, it emerges from *Re Ralli's WT* (1963) that the rule in *Strong v Bird* (1874) applies by analogy so that T will be able to enforce the trust on B's behalf. (Contrast, however, with *Re Brook* (1939).)

(3) Where X contracts with Y that, when Y dies, X will confer a benefit on B and in due course Y's estate becomes vested in B as his personal representative, it appears from *Beswick v Beswick* (1968) that B can then enforce the benefit against X.

Property	Mode of transfer
Legal estates in land (that is, freeholds/leases for three or more years):	By deed (s 52 of the LPA 1925)
Chattels:	By delivery (note, in particular, *Re Cole* (1964)) or by deed (see *Jaffa v Taylor Galleries* (1990))
Company shares:	By memorandum of transfer in the form contemplated by s 1 of the Stock Transfer Act 1963)/s 163 of the CA 1985, coupled with registration of shares. See: *Milroy v Lord; Trustee of Pehrsson's Property v Van Greyerz* (1999). But, note that the introduction of electronic share transfers in 1996 has meant that share transfer forms (but not registration) are now dispensed with in the case of certain plcs
Choses in action:	By assignment in accordance with the procedure in s 136 of the LPA
Equitable interests:	By disposition in writing (s 53(1)(c) of the LPA)

Circumstances in which a gift is enforceable without vesting

```
                    ┌──────────────────────────────┐
                    │  Enforcement without vesting  │
                    └──────────────────────────────┘
         ┌───────────────┬──────────┴──────┬───────────────┐
         ▼               ▼                 ▼               ▼
┌──────────────┐  ┌──────────────┐  ┌──────────────┐  ┌──────────────┐
│   Marriage   │  │     DMCs     │  │              │  │ Proprietary  │
│  settlement  │  │              │  │              │  │  estoppel    │
└──────────────┘  └──────────────┘  └──────────────┘  └──────────────┘
         ▼                                   ▼
┌─────────────────────────┐      ┌─────────────────────────┐
│ Damages for breach of   │      │  Trust of covenant to   │
│  covenant to settle     │      │        settle           │
└─────────────────────────┘      └─────────────────────────┘
```

Marriage settlements

Where S promises to settle property on T pursuant to a marriage settlement and the marriage takes place but vesting does not occur, equity allows T to enforce the trust on behalf of the spouses and their issue: see *Pullan v Koe* (1913). The reason for this is that equity regards the spouses and issue as having given notional consideration by virtue of the marriage.

The children of either spouse from an earlier marriage are also deemed to fall within the marriage consideration, provided the interest of such children are closely linked with those of the issue of the marriage: see *AG v Jacobs-Smith* (1895).

Where the marriage settlement provides that the property is to pass to the next-of-kin or some other third party if the spouses die without issue, such a party does not come within the marriage consideration. The trustees cannot therefore enforce the trust on his behalf where vesting has not occurred: see *Re D'Angibau* (1880); *Re Plumptre's Marriage Settlement* (1910) and *Re Pryce* (1917).

Enforcement of covenants to settle under the common law

A covenant is a promise to transfer property which is under seal. Equity will not enforce the covenant by decreeing specific performance if it is not supported by consideration: see *Jeffreys v Jeffreys* (1841); *Re D'Angibau* and *Re Ellenborough* (1903).

By contrast, the common law will enforce the covenant against the covenantor without requiring consideration from the covenantee. For example, if A and B execute a voluntary deed under which A covenants to transfer property belonging to him to B, but fails to transfer it, B may recover damages against him: see *Cannon v Hartley* (1949).

The position is less certain where a settlor, S, covenants to transfer property to a trustee, T, to hold on trust for B. It has been decided in cases like *Re Pryce* (1917); *Re Kay* (1939) and *Re Cook* (1965), that where the covenant is not performed, B cannot compel T to bring an action for damages while T for his part will be directed by the court not to do so.

By contrast, in *Re Cavendish-Browne* (1916), which was decided shortly before *Re Pryce*, the court allowed T to claim damages on behalf of B, for the breach of a voluntary covenant by S to settle property left to her under two wills.

The decision in *Re Cavendish-Browne*, however, raises some difficulties:

- in so far as T would not be beneficially entitled to the trust property if it had been transferred pursuant to the covenant, it is arguable that he should be awarded no more than nominal damages;

- even if T can be awarded substantial damages, it would hardly be appropriate for him to claim beneficial ownership of the amount awarded. At the same time, B would still require the assistance which equity has already withheld in order to compel T to hold the damages on trust for him (B). If neither T nor B is thus beneficially entitled to the amount awarded, it follows that the beneficial vacuum would be filled by requiring T to hold on resulting trust for S, thus rendering such an award futile.

Enforcement in equity where there is a trust of the covenant
Where there is a voluntary covenant by S to settle property on T on trust for B, T may be not be willing to enforce the covenant. B may, however, be able to do so if he shows that S intended the right to sue on the covenant to be held on trust for B. In this event, the right to sue is treated as a *chose in action* and the trust of this *chose in action* becomes completely constituted when the covenant is made, even if the property which S covenanted to settle on trust has not yet been transferred to T.

This principle was established in *Fletcher v Fletcher* (1844) where B was able to enforce a covenant by S to settle £60,000 on T on trust for B. It has, however, subsequently been held in *Re Cook* that even if a trust of a covenant is enforceable where it relates to specific property or a sum of money, this will not be the case where it concerns future property.

A donatio mortis causa (DMC)
A DMC is a gift made in the donor's lifetime but expressed to be conditional on and intended to take effect on his death. It is neither an *inter vivos* gift in the strict sense, nor is it a testamentary gift which must comply with the formalities laid down in the Wills Act: see *Re Beaumont* (1902).

According to Russell CJ in *Cain v Moon* (1896), three conditions must exist for a DMC to be valid:

(1) the gift must be in contemplation of the donor's death;

(2) the donor must intend the property to revert to him if he does not die; and

(3) the subject matter of the DMC (or the means of gaining control of it) must be delivered to the donee.

Where the subject matter is a chattel and it has been delivered to the donee or trustee or he has been given the means of gaining access to it (such as the key to the place where it is kept), the donor's death perfects the gift: see, for example, *Woodard v Woodard* (1991).

If the subject matter is such that delivery would not suffice to constitute an *inter vivos* transfer, title to the property will not vest automatically in the donee/trustee on the donor's death but will pass to his personal representative. Equity will, however, perfect the gift by compelling the personal representative to complete the transfer: see, for example, *Re Mead* (1880) (gift of negotiable instrument); *Birch v Treasury Solicitor* (1951) (gift of money in deposit account) and *Sen v Headley* (1991) (gift of donor's house).

Enforcement under the doctrine of proprietary estoppel

If a property owner (O) by his words or conduct represents to another person (P) that P is entitled to an interest in the property, thereby inducing P to act to his detriment, O is *estopped* in equity from denying the truth of the representation.

Estoppel has been invoked in cases where a landowner has made an incomplete transfer of an interest in land and the transferee has relied to his detriment on the belief that the transfer is effective. In such circumstances, equity will compel the owner to transfer the property or do whatever else is necessary to give effect to the transferee's interest: see *Dillwyn v Llewellyn* (1862) and *Pascoe v Turner* (1979).

3 Resulting and constructive trusts

Resulting trusts

In certain situations, trusts are capable of arising without having been specifically declared by a settlor. Such trusts may either be resulting or constructive. Both types of trust are accorded statutory recognition in s 53(2) of the LPA which provides that they need not comply with the same formalities as express trusts.

Nature and types of resulting trusts

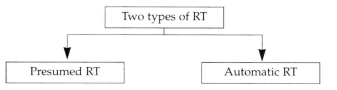

Where one party (A) transfers or directs property to which he is beneficially entitled to be transferred to another party (B), without declaring that B is to hold it on trust for A, equity sometimes imposes on B a resulting trust in A's favour.

The significance of intention in relation to resulting trusts
Resulting trusts have traditionally been imposed on the basis of the *presumption* that in undertaking the transfer, A did not *intend* B to take beneficially. In this connection, it has been pointed out by Potter LJ in *Twinsectra v Yardley* (1999) that:

... whereas express trusts are fundamentally dependent on the settlor's intention to create a trust, the role of intention in resulting trusts is a negative one, the essential question being whether or not the provider intended to benefit the recipient and not whether he or she intended to create a trust.

The basic premise that resulting trusts invariably depend on presumed intention was challenged by Megarry J in *Re Vandervell's Trusts (No 2)* where he identified two distinct species of resulting trusts, namely:

(1) *presumed resulting trusts*: which arise where there is a voluntary transfer of property or a purchase in the name of another; and

(2) *automatic resulting trusts*: which arise in situations where there is a vacuum in beneficial ownership and 'do not depend on any intentions or presumptions'– *per* Megarry VC in *Re Vandervell*.

This distinction between automatic and presumed resulting trusts has been called into question by Lord Browne-Wilkinson in *Westdeutsche Landesbank Girozentrale v Islington LBC* (1994). Lord Browne-Wilkinson's criticism centres on Megarry J's assertion that automatic resulting trusts did not depend on intention. The substance of Lord Browne-Wilkinson's argument is that, even in those situations where a vacuum in beneficial ownership would be characterised by Megarry J as giving rise to an automatic resulting trust, intention was still material since a resulting trust would be excluded if the settlor expressly or impliedly intended to abandon his beneficial interest. In such an event, the beneficial vacuum would be filled by passing the interest to the Crown as *bona vacantia*.

Despite Lord Browne-Wilkinson's stance, Megarry J's twofold classification into presumed and automatic resulting trusts remains useful for expository purposes and is still adopted in most leading texts.

Presumed resulting trusts

SUMMARY	
1 Circumstances in which RTs will be presumed:	
(a) voluntary transfer of personalty	Yes
(b) voluntary transfer of realty	Uncertain (s 60(3) of the LPA)
(c) purchase in another's name (realty/personalty)	Yes
2 Presumption of RT yields to presumption of advancement in favour of:	
(a) wife of transferor/purchaser	
(b) legitimate child where tansferor/purchaser is the father	
(c) person in respect of whom transferor stands *in loco parentis*	
3 Both presumptions may be rebutted by evidence of contrary intention	
But note:	
– where the evidence relied on discloses an illegal purpose, it is inadmissible to rebut presumption of advancement;	
– where a claim is founded on the presumption of RT, evidence of illegality has no bearing on the claim	

Voluntary transfer of property

Where A transfers property (whether real or personal) to B who furnishes consideration, there is no basis for a resulting trust to be presumed. See *Winstanley v Winstanley* (1999).

Where A transfers *personal property* owned by him to B for no consideration, a resulting trust for A is presumed unless B proves that A intended an outright gift to him: see *Standing v Bowring* (1885); *Re Vinogradoff* (1935); *Re Muller* (1953) and *Thavorn v BCCI* (1985).

Before 1925, a resulting trust was also presumed in the case of a voluntary conveyance of *real property*. The position has now been made uncertain by the provision in s 60(3) of the LPA 1925 that, *'in a voluntary conveyance, a resulting trust for the grantor shall not be implied, merely by reason that the property is not expressed to be for the use or benefit of the grantee'*.

Some writers suggest that the effect of s 60(3) is that, on a voluntary conveyance of land, a resulting trust will no longer be presumed but will only be imposed if there is evidence that this was the grantor's intention: see, for example, Snell, Pettitt, Chambers and the Law Commission's 1999 Consultation Paper on *Illegal Transactions*. Others maintain that s 60(3) does not preclude a resulting trust from being presumed on general equitable principles. See, for example, Hanbury and Martin; Parker and Mellows.

Judges, like Russell LJ (in *Hodgson v Marks* (1971)) and Lord Browne-Wilkinson (in *Tinsley v Milligan* (1993)), have also remarked on the difficulty inherent in construing s 60(3), but have not gone further to clarify the legal position.

Purchase in another's name

Personal property: Where A purchases *personal property* in B's name, there is a presumed resulting trust in A's favour: see *Fowkes v Pascoe* (1875); *Shephard v Cartwright* (1955); and *Crane v Davis* (1981).

Real property: Where A provides the money for the purchase of *real property* (whether freehold or leasehold) and directs that it should be conveyed or assigned to B or put in B's name, B is presumed to hold it on a resulting trust for A: see *Dyer v Dyer* (1788); *Pettitt v Pettitt* (1970) and *Gross v French* (1975).

Contributions: A resulting trust may arise where A and B both contribute towards purchasing property. In particular:

- If A and B contribute towards the purchase of property which is conveyed to B, B holds the legal title on resulting trust for A proportionate to his contribution: see *Bull v Bull* (1955); *Dewar v Dewar* (1975); *Sekhon v Alissa* (1989); *Tinsley v Milligan* (1993) and *Garvin-Mack v Garvin-Mack* (1993).

- If A and B contribute towards property which is put in their joint names, there will be a presumed resulting trust with each party's equitable interest being proportionate to his contribution: see *Springette v Defoe* (1992) and *Tagoe v Layea* (1993).

- If property is purchased in A's name by means of a mortgage and the liability for paying off the mortgage falls on A and B, a resulting trust will be presumed in B's favour in proportion to his liability: see *Moate v Moate* (1948); *Cowcher v Cowcher* (1972).

- A resulting trust will not, however, arise where B's contribution to property purchased in A's name is merely intended as a loan. See *Re Sharpe* (1980); *Clark v Manjot* (1998).

The presumption of advancement

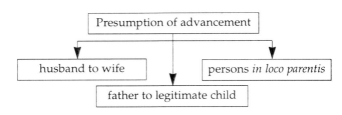

Where A transfers property to B or purchases property in B's name, in circumstances where the presumption of advancement applies, A will be deemed to have intended to make an outright gift to B, unless there is evidence of a contrary intention. This presumption arises in three contexts:

(a) *Husband to wife:* The operation of this presumption where a husband transfers property to his wife or purchases property in her name is illustrated by cases like *Re Eykyn's Trusts* (1877); *Thornley v Thornley* (1893); *Gascoigne v Gascoigne* (1918); and *Tinker v Tinker* (1970). This presumption has, however, never been extended to a man's mistress: see *Soar v Foster* (1858); *Diwell v Farnes* (1959); and *Garvin-Mack v Garvin-Mack* (1993). Moreover, the presumption does not arise where property is purchased or transferred into a husband's name by his wife. See *Heseltine v Heseltine* (1975); *Abrahams v Trustees of the Property of Abrahams* (1999).

In recent decades, wives have become considerably less economically dependent on their husbands than they were when the presumption was conceived. In recognition of this, it has been suggested in *Silver v Silver* (1958) and *Pettitt v Pettitt* that, although the wife's presumption has not been dispensed with, it ought to be accorded less weight than it was in by-gone years.

(b) *Father to legitimate child:* The relationship between a father and his legitimate child has long given rise to a presumption of advancement: see *Lord Grey v Lady Grey* (1677); *Crabb v Crabb* (1834); *Re Roberts* (1946); and *Shephard v Cartwright* (1955). *Note*, however, *McGrath v Wallis* (1995) which suggests that the courts are now considerably less inclined to rely on this presumption than they were in the past.

There is no corresponding presumption as between mother and child (see *Re De Visme* (1863); *Bennet v Bennet* (1879)) and *Ward v Snelling* (1994); though it was stated in *Bennet* that 'in the case of a mother ... it is easier to prove a gift ... very little evidence beyond the gift is wanted, there being very little motive required to induce a mother to make a gift to her child'.

(c) *Persons in loco parentis:* Where A assumes the position of B's lawful father, A is said to be *in loco parentis*: see *ex parte Pye* (1811). If A transfers property to B or purchases property in B's name, a presumption of advancement will arise in B's favour: see *Ebrand v Dancer* (1680) (grandfather-grandchild); *Re Paradise Motor Co* (1968) (stepfather-stepson); and *Beckford v Beckford* (1774) (father-illegitimate child).

Rebutting the presumptions

Where A transfers property to B or purchases property in B's name, the onus of rebutting the presumption of resulting trust rests with B. He may do so either:

- by proving that the relationship between the parties is one which raises a presumption of advancement in B's favour; or

- by giving evidence of the acts or declarations of either party or of other circumstances which indicate that A wished to confer a beneficial interest on B. Such evidence was found to exist in cases like *Fowkes v Pascoe* (1875); *Standing v Bowring*; *Ward v Snelling*; and *Bradbury v Hoolin* (1998).

Conversely, where A transfers property to B or purchases property in B's name and the operative presumption is of advancement, the onus is on A to rebut this presumption. Again, this may be done by evidence relating to acts and declarations of the parties or the circumstances surrounding the transfer. Cases in which this presumption was rebutted include *Lord Grey v Lady Grey*; *Scawin v Scawin* (1841); *Warren v Gurney* (1944); *Marshall v Crutwell* (1875); *Simpson v Simpson* (1992); and *McGrath v Wallis*.

The rules in Shephard v Cartwright

Where the evidence adduced to rebut either presumption consists of acts or declarations, the case of *Shephard v Cartwright* lays down two rules, namely that:

(1) acts/declarations made *before* or *at the time of* the transfer or purchase are admissible either *for* or *against* the maker; while

(2) acts/declarations made *after* the transfer or purchase has been concluded are admissible in evidence only *against* the maker.

Evidence of illegal conduct

```
            ┌─────────────────────────────┐
            │  Transfer/purchase in another's │
            │      name for illegal purpose   │
            └─────────────────────────────┘
                 │                      │
                 ▼                      ▼
```

Where there is a presumption of advancement:	Where there is a presumption of RT:
• Evidence disclosing illegal purpose is not ordinarily admissible to rebut the presumption. (See *Gascoigne v Gascoigne* (1918), etc.) • But, such evidence is admissible where the party relying on it withdraws from the transaction before carrying it into effect. (See *Tribe v Tribe* (1995).)	Presumption will be upheld in spite of the illegal purpose since the party in whose favour the presumption exists need not rely on the illegality. (See *Tinsley v Milligan* (1993), etc.)

Where, in furtherance of some illegal purpose, A purchases property in B's name or transfers property to B, the 'reliance principle' comes into play. The effect of this principle depends on whether the purchase or transfer is one which gives rise to the presumption of advancement or of resulting trust.

(a) The presumption of advancement

Where A transfers property to B (who happens to be his wife or child) in pursuance of an illegal purpose (for example, to defraud a third party), A can only rebut the presumption of advancement in B's favour by relying on evidence of the illegal purpose. Cases such as *Gascoigne v Gascoigne* (1918); *Re Emery's Investment* (1959), *Chettair v Chettair* (1962) and *Tinker v Tinker* (1970) have decided that A will not be allowed to adduce evidence of this illegal purpose and, in effect, will not be able to claim the property beneficially.

The Court of Appeal has, however, held in *Tribe v Tribe* (1995) that a father, who transferred shares to his son in order to escape liability under impending litigation, could rely on this evidence to rebut the presumption of advancement where he withdrew from the illegal purpose before it was carried into effect. This has recently been affirmed *per obiter* by Nourse LJ in *Eeles v Williams* (1998).

(b) The presumption of resulting trust

Where A has purchased property in B's name or transferred property to B (who is not his wife or child), it has been held in *Tinsley v Milligan* that the fact that this was done in pursuance of an illegal purpose will not deprive A of his beneficial interest. This is because a presumption or resulting trust arises in A's favour which means that he need not adduce any evidence and so has no need to rely on the illegal purpose to establish his entitlement. See, also, *Silverwood v Silverwood* (1997); *Lowson v Combes* (1998); and *Eeles v Williams*.

The fact that A can assert his beneficial interest in property which he puts in B's name where there is a presumption of resulting trust but not where there is a presumption of advancement has led to some criticism of the reliance principle by academic commentators like Martin and Penner, as well as in cases such as *Silverwood v Silverwood* (Nourse LJ) and *Tribe v Tribe* (Judge Weekes). Nourse LJ declares, for instance, that:

> ... it is not easy to understand or to see any public or other policy or advantage behind a rule which regulates a claimant's right to recover solely according to whether the transfer is to his child or wife ... on the one hand or his brother, grandchild or anyone else on the other.

Similar sentiments have recently been expressed in the Law Commission Consultation Paper on *Illegal Transactions*, which states that such arbitrariness is difficult to defend and offers a powerful argument for reform in this area.

Automatic resulting trusts

	Summary	
1	Express trust not effectively declared	Property held on resulting trust for settlor
2	Failure of express trust because stipulated condition is not fulfilled	Property held on resulting trust for settlor
3	Failure of express trust to dispose of entire beneficial interest	Undisposed interest held in resulting trust for settlor
4	Surplus left after trust purpose has been accomplished	Three possible outcomes: – trustee takes surplus – resulting trust of surplus for settlor/contributors – gift treated as absolute with surplus passing to intended beneficiaries
5	Surplus left after dissolution of an unincorporated association	Two possible outcomes: – resulting trust of surplus for all the members in proportion to their contributions – distribution determined by the terms of the contract between those who were members at the time of dissolution
6	Money advanced for a purpose but can no longer be applied for that purpose	*Quistclose*-type resulting trust in favour of party who advanced the money
7	Money paid out in connection with a purpose/scheme which turns out to be *ultra vires*	CA decided in the *Westdeutsche* case that there would be a resulting trust of the money. Resulting trust held not to arise on further appeal to HoL

As Lord Diplock declared in *Vandervell v IRC* (1967), 'equity abhors a beneficial vacuum'. Accordingly, where S transfers property to T under a trust which leaves some or all of the beneficial interest undisposed of, equity automatically fills the vacuum by requiring T to hold the outstanding equitable interest on a resulting trust for S. The main contexts in which such resulting trusts arise are as follows:

(1) Where property passes to T under an express trust which is not effectively declared: see *Re Keen* (1937) and *Re Vandervell (No 2)* (1974).

(2) Where an express trust fails, because it is subject to a condition which is not fulfilled as in *Re Ames' Settlement* (1946).

(3) Where a trust fails to dispose of the whole beneficial interest, such as where S gives Blackacre to T on trust for B for life without stating what will happen when B dies. This is often due to bad drafting and as Harman LJ remarked in *Re Cochrane* (1955) 'a resulting trust is the last resort to which the law has recourse when the draftsman has made a blunder'.

(4) *The position where a surplus is left in the trust fund after its purpose has been fulfilled*: In such an event, unless it is established that the settlor/testator intended the trustee to retain the surplus, two possibilities emerge from the decided cases:

(i) In one line of cases, the courts have held that the beneficiaries were not entitled to the whole fund absolutely but only to so much of it as was needed for the specified purpose so that, once the purpose is fulfilled, there will be a resulting trust of the surplus. See *Re Sanderson's Trust* (1851) (trust fund for upkeep of testator's imbecile brother) and *Re the Trust of the Abbott*

Fund (1900) (trust fund for the upkeep of two deaf and dumb ladies). After the deaths of the beneficiaries, in both cases there was a resulting trust of the surplus in their respective funds.

(ii) The opposite conclusion was reached in *Re Andrew's Trust* (1905) (trust fund to educate children of deceased clergymen) and *Re Osoba* (1979) (trust of testator's residuary estate to educate his daughter up to university level). In these cases, the court regarded the specified purpose as no more than the motive for the gift and held that the respective beneficiaries were absolutely entitled to the trust fund and could claim the surplus after their education. This reasoning has been adopted in *Davis v Hardwick* (1999). Here, the people of a village raised a trust fund to enable a child born in the village to undergo pioneering liver transplant surgery and there was a substantial surplus after treatment was completed. It was held that the beneficiary was entitled to the fund absolutely and not only to so much of it as was required for his treatment.

(5) *The position where an unincorporated association ceases to exist*: Where this occurs, the association's surplus funds are sometimes dealt with by imposing a resulting trust in favour of the contributors: see, for example, *Re Printers and Transferrers Society* (1899); *Re Hobourn Aero Components, etc, Fund* (1946); *Davis v Richards and Wallington Industries* (1990); and *Air Jamaica v Charlton* (1999).

In other cases, however, the courts have favoured a contractual approach. The substance of this approach is that the constitution or other body of rules of an incorporated association constitutes a contract which binds all its members and it is this contract which should determine what will happen to the association's surplus funds in the event of dissolution. This approach has been adopted with varying results in a host of cases, such as *Cunnack v Edwards* (1896); *Re West Sussex Constabulary, etc, Fund Trusts* (1971); *Re Sick and Funeral Society of St John's Sunday School, Golcar* (1973); *Re Bucks Constabulary Friendly Society (No 2)* (1979); and *Re GKN Bolts and Nuts Club* (1982).

(6) *The position where money is made available for a stated purpose but can no longer be applied for that purpose*: It emerges from the cases of *Barclays Bank v Quistclose Investments* (1970), *Carreras Rothman v Freeman Mathews Treasure* (1985) and *Re EVTR* (1987) that this will give rise to a resulting trust. The effect of this 'Quistclose-type' resulting trust is that the party into whose hands the money was paid will be obliged to hold it on trust for the party who made the money available in the first place. However, where such a payment is made without being required to be set apart and applied for a particular purpose, it will not be subject to a *Quistclose*-type trust. See *Guardian Ocean Cargoes v Banco do Brasil* (1994).

(7) *The position where money is paid for a purpose which turns out to be* ultra vires: In the *Westdeutsche* case, a bank paid money to a local authority (LA) under an interest swap agreement which was subsequently declared *ultra vires*. The Court of Appeal found the LA liable to make restitution of these payments which were made for no consideration not only at law but also in equity; and held that, even though the legal title to the money had passed to the LA, equitable title remained in the bank. In effect, the LA held the money on resulting trust for the bank. This decision accorded with the thesis advanced by Birks in his essay on Restitution and

Resulting Trusts, which put forward a case for a wider role for the resulting trust in the field of restitution and, particularly, in cases of mistake and failure of consideration.

The decision has, however, been overturned by the House of Lords which held that the payments made by the bank under the void transaction were recoverable at law as money had and received but not held on resulting trust by the recipient LA. In his lead judgment, Lord Browne-Wilkinson, having alluded to Birk's thesis, signified that he was more persuaded by the counter argument put forward by Swadling in his article 'A new role for resulting trusts?' and declared that 'to impose a resulting trust in such circumstances is inconsistent with the traditional principles of trusts law'.

Constructive trusts

The general nature of constructive trusts
As explained by Edmund-Davies LJ in *Carl Zeiss Stiftung v Smith (No 2)* (1969):

> English law has no clear cut all embracing definition of the constructive trust ... Its boundaries have been left perhaps deliberately vague so as not to restrict the court by technicalities in deciding what the justice of a particular case may require.

This is not entirely surprising given that the constructive trust is the residual category of trust which according to Hanbury and Martin 'is called into play where a court desires to impose a trust and no other suitable category exists'.

According to leading textbooks (for example, Hanbury, Pettitt and Snell), the most significant attribute of constructive trusts is that they arise by operation of law in the sense that they are imposed by equity regardless of the intention of the property owner.

The place of the remedial constructive law in English law

In English law, the constructive trust is traditionally viewed as a *substantive institution* in much the same way as an express or resulting trust. As thus conceived, constructive trusts operate in a limited number of well defined situations to vindicate pre-existing proprietary rights. According to this view, the constructive trust comes into being when the facts which activate the operation of law occur and is therefore binding on third parties from that time and not from the time the trust is upheld in any ensuing litigation.

In the United States, the constructive trust is regarded not as a substantive institution but as an *equitable remedy* which may be pursued in court against a defendant who unjustly enriches himself by acquiring or retaining property at the plaintiff's expense. As thus conceived, it is awarded in order to compel the defendant to convey the property to the plaintiff rather than to hold it on trust as such. A notable feature of the remedial constructive trust is its flexibility. Instead of being confined to certain well established situations like the institutional constructive trust, it has a wider remit as 'the formula through which the conscience of equity finds expression', *per* Cardozo J in *Beatty v Guggenheim Exploration* (1919).

Emergence of the new model constructive trust

The American example inspired the creation of the *new model constructive trust* as a vehicle for extending the frontiers of the constructive trust beyond its traditional limits. The assumption underlying this new model approach was that a constructive trust ought to be imposed 'whenever justice and good conscience require it', *per* Lord Denning in *Hussey v Palmer* (1972).

Main spheres of application of the new model constructive trust

The influence of the new model trust has been most perceptible:

- in disputes between spouses/co-habitees over family property: see, for example, *Cooke v Head* (1972) and *Eves v Eves* (1975);

- in the sphere of contractual licences: see, in particular, *Binions v Evans* (1972).

Criticisms of the new model constructive trust

The new model constructive trust was, however, subjected to sustained criticisms by academic commentators, such as Maudsley, Oakley and Hayton. These have been reinforced in the judicial sphere by the remarks of Bagnall J in *Cowcher v Cowcher* (1973).

The two main criticisms levelled against the new model approach are:

- that the emphasis it places on fairness and justice makes it unduly subjective. This is considered particularly undesirable in disputes over property rights which are best dealt with on the basis of sure and settled principles; and

- that, in concentrating on doing justice between the parties to the dispute, it does not take sufficient account of the interests of third parties which might be adversely affected by imposing a constructive trust.

In view of these concerns, the courts have since the 1980s been reluctant to extend the new model trust into new areas. Even in those areas in which it was invoked in the past, the courts have circumscribed the new model constructive trust by insisting that it will not be imposed arbitrarily but within well-defined limits and in accordance with settled principles. Accordingly:

- in disputes over the family home, a constructive trust will no longer be imposed, just because the judge thinks this is fair to the claimant. Both partners must have a common intention that the claimant should have an interest in the property and there must be detrimental reliance on the claimant's part: see, for example, *Burns v Burns* (1984); *Grant v Edwards* (1986); and *Lloyd's Bank v Rosset* (1991);

- again, in the sphere of contractual licences, the courts are now entirely more circumspect about imposing constructive trusts. This is discernible from *Ashburn Anstalt v Arnold* (1989), where the Court of Appeal made it clear that not all licensees would be protected by a constructive trust. In the court's view, it was not desirable 'that constructive trusts of land should be imposed on inferences drawn from slender material'.

Although the influence of the new model constructive trust has now waned, the broader issue of whether the remedial constructive trust has any place within contemporary English law has not yet been decisively settled.

On the one hand, Lord Millett has asserted extra-judicially that 'there is neither room nor need for the remedial constructive trust'; while Birks describes it as 'an object of suspicion'. This aversion to the remedial constructive trust is also evident in cases like *Halifax BS v Thomas* (1996).

Here, HBS lent money to T to buy a house on the strength of T's fraudulent representation regarding his financial standing. The house was later sold and HBS was paid in full out of the proceeds of sale leaving a surplus. HBS sought to claim this surplus contending that a constructive trust should be imposed to prevent T from unjustly enriching himself by retaining it. In rejecting this claim, the Court of Appeal made it clear that, in English law, the constructive trust had not become a remedy for unjust enrichment. See, also, *Re Polly Peck (No 2)* (1999) where the court was equally resistant to the remedial constructive trust.

There are, however, other cases in which the courts have acknowledged the possibility that the remedial constructive trust may yet have a role to play in the realm of English property law. In *Metall und Rohstoff AC v Donaldson Lufkin* (1990), for instance, it was stated that there is 'a good arguable case' that circumstances may arise in which the court can impose a remedial constructive trust. More recently, in the *Westdeutsche* case, Lord Browne-Wilkinson alluded to the prospect that:

> ... the court by way of remedy might impose a constructive trust on a defendant who knowingly retains property of which the plaintiff has been unjustly deprived.

As his Lordship went on to point out, however:

> ... whether English law should follow the United States and Canada by adopting the remedial constructive trust will have to be decided in some future case where the point is directly in issue.

Traditional constructive trusts

Long before the new model approach was conceived, constructive trusts were traditionally recognised in a variety of contexts. Some of these contexts are dealt with below.

Constructive trusts in the context of fiduciary relationships

Equity has long sought to ensure that a fiduciary does not allow his interests to conflict with his duty: see *Bray v Ford* (1896).

It has been observed in cases like *Re Coomber* (1911) and *English v Dedham Vale Properties* (1978) that fiduciary relationships are many and varied and new types are capable of arising from time to time. As explained in *Reading v AG* (1951), such a relationship exists whenever one party entrusts another with a job to perform. Its key feature is that one party (the principal) reposes confidence in another (the fiduciary). Elaborating on this, Millett LJ stated in *Bristol and West BS v Mathew* (1996) that:

> ... a fiduciary is someone who has undertaken to act for or on behalf of another in a particular manner in circumstances which give rise to a relationship of trust and confidence. The distinguishing obligation of a fiduciary is the obligation of loyalty. The principal is entitled to the single-minded loyalty of his [fiduciary].

A fiduciary will be liable as a constructive trustee in the following circumstances:

(1) *Where he receives remuneration to which he is not entitled:* this will be the case where he either:

- makes unauthorised payments to himself or accepts unauthorised payments out of his principal's funds (see

TRUSTS LAW

Chapter 5, p 125, for a discussion of what constitutes authorised payments/remuneration); or

- appropriates to himself payments received from third parties to which the principal is entitled: see *Sugden v Crossland* (1856); *Erlanger v New Sombrero Phosphate* (1878); *Williams v Barton* (1927); *Re Macadam* (1945); and *Guiness v Saunders* (1990).

(2) *Where he enters into a transaction on his own behalf which he should have done on his principal's behalf:* This is exemplified by:

- The rule in *Keech v Sandford* (1726): which established that where trust property includes a leasehold interest, the trustee is bound on the expiry of the term to seek a renewal on behalf of the trust. If he renews the lease (or acquires the leasehold reversion) for himself, he will be obliged to hold it on constructive trust for the beneficiaries: see *Keech v Sandford* and *Protheroe v Protheroe* (1968).

   This rule has been extended to other fiduciaries; for example, personal representatives, agents and partners: see, for example, *Re Biss* (1903).

- The decision in *Regal (Hastings) v Gulliver* (1942): This case re-affirmed in a different context the principle in *Keech v Sandford*. R Ltd wished to lease two cinemas through a subsidiary, A Ltd. To facilitate the grant of the leases, directors of R Ltd, without authorisation from the shareholders paid for £3,000 shares in A Ltd. When R Ltd was sold they profited personally from their stake in A Ltd. It was held that they must account as constructive trustees of these profits to the new owners of R Ltd: see, also, *Industrial Development Consultants v Cooley* (1980); but note the more flexible approach adopted in

Commonwealth cases like *Peso Silver Mines v Cropper* (1966) (Canada) and *Queensland Mines v Hudson* (1978) (Australia).

(3) *Where he uses confidential information for his own ends:* The position in this regard is well illustrated by *Boardman v Phipps* (1967), where B, a solicitor to a trust, and TP, one of the beneficiaries, utilised information and opportunities which came their way through their connection with the trust to take control of a company in which the trust had a sizeable shareholding. It was held that they were liable as constructive trustees for the profits which they had made in the process.

The position is, however, different when one party (A) is in a fiduciary relationship with another (B) and as a result of A's breach of his fiduciary duty, a third party (C), who does not stand in a fiduciary position to B, acquires a business opportunity. The Court of Appeal has held in *Satnam Investments Ltd v Dunlop Heywood Ltd* (1998) that, in such an event, C will not be liable to B as a constructive trustee.

(4) *Where he receives a bribe:* The Court of Appeal decided in *Lister v Stubbs* (1890) that, where a fiduciary accepts a bribe, he does not hold it as a constructive trustee. As such, his aggrieved principal will have a personal claim emanating from the fiduciary's liability to account for the amount received but not a proprietary claim against him: see, also, *Powell and Thomas v Evans Jones* (1905); and *Iran Shipping Lines v Denby* (1987).

This differentiation between a personal liability to account and the imposition of a constructive trust is significant at two levels:

- in the event of the fiduciary's insolvency, the principal

would be accorded priority over the fiduciary's other creditors in respect of property held on constructive trust but not funds/property which is subject to a liability to account;

• in the event of an increase in value of the property in the fiduciary's hands, the principal would be able to claim the benefit of the increase if held on constructive trust but not if there is only a personal liability to account.

Over the years, various commentators have criticised the decision in *Lister v Stubbs*. In particular, Oakley and Hayton considered it anomalous that a patently dishonest fiduciary who took bribes would merely be affixed with personal liability while other fiduciaries who profited from their position without acting dishonestly had been declared constructive trustees in cases such as *Williams v Barton*; *Regal (Hastings) v Gulliver* and *Boardman v Phipps*.

In the New Zealand case of *AG (Hong Kong) v Reid* (1994), the Privy Council sought to correct this anomaly by departing from *Lister* and holding that a Crown Servant who had bought property with bribes received in the course of his employment was a constructive trustee of the property.

The conclusion in *Reid* that a bribe-taking fiduciary is a constructive trustee is not without its difficulties, especially where the principal seeks to assert a proprietary claim against other creditors of the fiduciary. See, for example, Watts' comment on this case in (1994) 110 LQR 178–80. Moreover, the decision in *Reid* is not binding on the English courts. It was endorsed by Lindsey J in *News International plc v Clinger* (1998), but the Court of Appeal declined to follow it in *Halifax BS v Thomas*.

Strangers as constructive trustees

• *Bona fide* purchaser for value • Innocent volunteer • Person dealing with property as agent	Not liable as constructive trustee
• Trustee *de son tort* • Accessory assisting in breach of trust • Person guilty of knowing receipt	Liable as constructive trustee

A trustee (or other fiduciary) who improperly allows property or funds entrusted to him to fall into the hands of strangers will be liable for any loss occasioned to the beneficiaries. Where the trustee cannot make good the loss, it has to be determined whether the stranger will be liable as a constructive trustee.

The stranger will not be liable as a constructive trustee:

• where he acquires trust property as a *bona fide* purchaser for value without notice: see *Pilcher v Rawlins* (1872);

• where he receives trust property as an innocent volunteer: in such an event, the beneficiary can trace the property into the hands of the recipient if it still exists in some traceable form. However, he is not in a fiduciary position *vis à vis* the beneficiary and will not be liable as a constructive trustee if the property passes out of his hands without his being aware of the trust: see *Re Diplock* (1948); *Re Montagu's ST* (1987); *Agip (Africa) v Jackson* (1992); and *Westdeutsche Landesbank v Islington LBC* (1994);

- where he is an agent of the trustee: trustees often delegate aspects of their responsibilities to agents like solicitors, stockbrokers, valuers and entrust trust property to such agents. The general rule in this regard is that an agent of the trust who acted honestly in the performance of his agency will not be liable for losses occasioned to the trust estate: see *Lee v Sankey* (1873); *Barnes v Addy* (1874); *Mara v Browne* (1896) and *Williams-Ashman v Price and Williams* (1942).

Situations in which a stranger will be a constructive trustee

A stranger who deals with trust property (including an agent) will be liable as a constructive trustee in three contexts, notably:

- where he is a *trustee de son tort*;

- where he is an *accessory*; or

- where he is a *recipient* of such property.

(1) The trustee de son tort

Cases like *Mara v Browne* establish that, if a person who is not a trustee and has no authority from the trustee becomes involved in administering the trust estate, he is a trustee *de son tort*. This makes him liable as a constructive trustee for the trust assets as well as for any loss occasioned by him. See, also, *James v Williams* (1999) where a constructive trust was imposed on a defendant who had administered an intestate estate without a grant and had acted throughout as if he was solely entitled to the estate.

(2) Accessory liability

Cases such as *Soar v Ashwell* (1893) and *Barnes v Addy* established the principle that a stranger who dishonestly assists a trustee (or other fiduciary) in a breach of duty would be liable as a constructive trustee for any loss occasioned by the breach.

In some instances, the stranger's role as an accessory will involve the *ministerial receipt* of property which he then deals with or disposes of in accordance with the fraudulent designs of the trustee/fiduciary (as happened in *Agip v Jackson*).

In other instances, the accessory's involvement will arise in circumstances which do not entail his receipt of property from the trustee. See, for example, *Eaves v Hickson* (1861) and Lord Browne-Wilkinson's judgment in the *Westdeutsche* case. In such circumstances, his liability to account will invariably be personal rather than proprietary. This has prompted various commentators (Pettitt, Martin, Birks, etc) to suggest that it is a misnomer to categorise him as a constructive trustee. This view has been echoed by Potter LJ in *Twinsectra v Yardley* (1999).

According to Peter Gibson J in *Baden Delvaux v Société Générale* (1983), accessory liability involves the following four elements:

(a) *The existence of a trust or other fiduciary relationship.*

(b) *The existence of a dishonest and fraudulent design on the part of the trustee/fiduciary*: Particular emphasis was laid on this requirement in cases like *Soar v Ashwell* and *Barnes v Addy*. It has, however, been held in *Royal Brunei Airlines v Tan* (1995) that this is not an essential requirement.

(c) *Assistance by the stranger*: In order for a stranger to be liable as an accessory, there must be some measure of participation on his part. Thus, for instance, in *Brinks Ltd v Abu-Saleh* (1995) where a wife had simply accompanied her husband on foreign holidays which he had used as a cover for money laundering operations, this did not render her liable.

(d) *Guilty knowledge on the part of the stranger*: In this context, the courts have recognised that knowledge has many shades of meaning. Peter Gibson J, himself, identified five possible categories of knowledge which could be ascribed to a stranger.

His first three categories (that is: (i) direct knowledge; (ii) deliberately averting one's eyes to the obvious; and (iii) wilful failure to make inquiries) are indicative of conscious impropriety or dishonesty on a stranger's part and categories (ii) and (iii) are thus treated on the same footing as actual knowledge. It has never been in doubt that these three categories of knowledge will render a stranger liable.

His last two categories (that is, knowledge of circumstances which would (iv) indicate the facts to a reasonable man; or (v) put an honest and reasonable man on inquiry) are generally regarded as tending more towards lack of care rather than dishonesty. Over the years, there has been a marked divergence of judicial opinion on the issue of whether a stranger could be affixed with liability on the strength of such negligence-based knowledge.

This issue has now been settled by the Privy Council in the *Royal Brunei* case, where Lord Nicholls conducted a detailed survey of the principles governing accessory liability and concluded that:

- dishonesty is a necessary ingredient of accessory liability;

- dishonesty is for the most part to be equated with conscious impropriety and carelessness is not dishonesty;

- 'knowingly' is best avoided as a defining ingredient in determining the liability of an accessory and the *Baden* scale of knowledge is best forgotten.

See, also, *Three Rivers DC v Governors of the Bank of England (No 3)* (1998).

(3) Recipient liability

A stranger who receives trust property for his own benefit, does not ordinarily take free from the trust, unless he is a *bona fide* purchaser for value without notice. He may thus be compelled to restore any property in his hands to the beneficiary, once he is affixed with notice of the trust, whether actual or constructive.

If the property is no longer in the recipient's hands, the beneficiary may still be able to proceed against him on the footing that he is under a personal liability to account in much the same way as an accessory. This has traditionally been characterised as liability for *'knowing receipt'* which points to the fact that a recipient would be affixed with liability only if he had some knowledge of the fact that the transfer was in breach of trust. There has, however, been some controversy regarding the degree of cognisance required.

On the one hand, in *Re Montagu's ST* (1987), Megarry VC insisted that a recipient would only be liable if he had actual knowledge of the *Baden (i)–(iii) categories.*

A contrary view was taken in the earlier case of *Karak Rubber v Burden (No 2)* (1972) where Brightman J held that a recipient would be liable if he had actual or constructive notice (the latter being akin to knowledge within the *Baden iv–v categories*). More recently, in cases like *Agip v Jackson* and

El Ajou v Dollar Holdings (1994), Millett LJ considered that a doctrine analogous to the doctrine of constructive notice had a place in the receipt cases which suggested to him that actual knowledge (within categories (i)–(iii)) was not a pre-condition for recipient liability.

A recent trend has been to re-characterise liability for knowing receipt as liability for unjust enrichment upon which a *restitutionary claim* can be founded. This is evident, for instance, in the New Zealand case of *Powell v Thompson* (1991) as well as in the *El Ajou* case and the *Royal Brunei* case. In *Powell*, Thomas J indicated that while accessory liability is based on unconscionable conduct, recipient liability is based on unjust enrichment. A similar distinction was drawn in *Royal Brunei* by Lord Nicholls who stated that 'recipient liability is restitution-based, accessory liability is not'. In similar vein, Millett LJ observed in *El Ajou* that:

> [Recipient liability] is the counterpart in equity of the common law action for money had and received. Both can be classified as receipt based restitutionary claims.

If this reasoning is accepted, it follows that the mere fact of receipt will ordinarily give rise to personal liability, even if the recipient is an innocent volunteer who is devoid of any knowledge or notice.

The movement away from knowing receipt as traditionally conceived in the direction of strict liability regardless of fault which is implicit in the restitutionary approach has not met with universal approval. This is borne out by Lord Browne-Wilkinson's endorsement of the traditional approach in the *Westdeutsche* case, where he declared that unless a third party recipient 'has the requisite degree of knowledge he is not personally liable to account as trustee'.

It remains to be seen which of these positions will ultimately prevail.

Resulting/constructive trusts in the context of the family home
Where a married or unmarried couple have set up home together, events such as the breakdown of the relationship or bankruptcy of either party may give rise to a dispute over their respective interests in the family home. Such a dispute may be settled: (1) under the Matrimonial Causes Act (MCA) 1973; (2) by giving effect to any *express declarations* made by the couple regarding their beneficial interests in the property; (3) by imposing a *resulting trust;* or (4) by imposing a *constructive trust.*

The MCA 1973
Where the dispute arises in the context of matrimonial proceedings, the MCA empowers the court to make whatever order is just and practicable regarding the property of both spouses without being bound by the strict rules of property law. Where the dispute falls outside the ambit of the MCA (for example, where it is between one spouse and a third party or where the partners are unmarried), the beneficial interests in the family home are determined under the general rules of property law. As Lord Diplock explained in *Gissing v Gissing* (1971), the operative principles in such cases are derived from the law of trusts.

Express declarations
If it is established that, at the time the property in dispute was acquired, the relevant conveyance expressly declared what beneficial interests each partner would have in the property, this will be the basis for determining their respective entitlements: see *Goodman v Gallant* (1986).

Where the legal title to the family home is conveyed to one partner and there is no formal declaration regarding the shares to be taken by each partner, such as would satisfy the requirement of s 53(1)(b) of the LPA, the other partner may be entitled to a beneficial interest in the property under a resulting trust or a constructive trust.

The imposition of a resulting trust

Where the property is in the male partner's name but the female partner contributed directly to the purchase price, a resulting trust will be presumed in her favour in proportion to her contribution immediately the property is vested in the man.

If the male partner contributes directly to the purchase price but the property is put in the name of the female partner, the position will depend on whether she is his wife or mistress:

- in the case of a mistress, a resulting trust will be presumed in favour of the contributing male partner; but

- in the case of a wife, there is a presumption of advancement and the onus is thus on the husband to prove that he did not intend an outright gift to her.

Where the legal title to the family home is in one partner's name, but the purchase was financed by a mortgage loan with both partners assuming the liability for repaying the loan, the partner to whom the legal title was conveyed will hold on resulting trust for both partners in proportion to their respective shares of the mortgage liability. See *Cowcher v Cowcher*; *Springette v Defoe*.

A claimant of an equitable interest in the family home who did not contribute to the initial purchase price or assume a share of the mortgage liability at the outset may seek to rely on (i) her subsequent financial contributions towards paying off the mortgage or (ii) her contributions towards family expenses, which enabled the partner with the legal title to repay the mortgage. Even though it was suggested by Fox LJ in *Burns v Burns* that contributions of this nature may give rise to a resulting trust in the claimant's favour, such claims are more appropriately dealt with in the realm of the constructive trust.

The imposition of a constructive trust

Constructive trusts have been imposed in disputes relating to the family home since the early 1970s when the two landmark cases of *Pettitt v Pettitt* and *Gissing v Gissing* were decided.

These cases established that where the legal title to the home is vested in one partner, a claim by the other to a beneficial share under a constructive trust will succeed if (1) there was a common intention that the claimant will acquire an interest in the home; and (2) the claimant has relied on this to his or her detriment.

In a later line of cases, which included *Cooke v Head* (1972), *Eves v Eves* (1975) and *Hall v Hall* (1982), Lord Denning's attachment to the new model approach led him to treat the constructive trust in this sphere purely as a discretionary formula for adjusting the property rights of spouses and co-habitees in order to achieve a fair and just solution between them.

The new model approach has lost momentum since Lord Denning relinquished judicial office and the courts have now reverted to the more orthodox principles laid down in *Gissing* and *Pettitt*, in cases such as *Burns v Burns* (1984), *Midland Bank v Dobson* (1986), *Grant v Edwards* (1986) and most decisively by the House of Lords in *Lloyd's Bank v Rosset*. These principles as articulated in *Rosset* have been reiterated and adopted in a host of subsequent cases such as *Hammond v Mitchell* (1991); *Springette v Defoe* (1992); *Midland Bank v Cooke* (1995) and *Clough v Kiley* (1996).

The notable effect of this reversion to orthodoxy is that a constructive trust will no longer be imposed on a co-habitee or spouse just because this is perceived to be fair and just, but can only be imposed where the requisite *common intention* and *detrimental reliance* are established.

(1) *Common intention:* it emerges from Lord Bridge's judgment in *Rosset* that the requisite common intention may be established either;

- by evidence of some express agreement, arrangement or understanding between the parties however imperfectly remembered and however imprecise its terms; or

- by inference from the conduct of the parties in cases where they have made direct contributions towards purchasing the property or paying the mortgage.

Note, however, that the position of a spouse/co-habitee, who relies on direct contributions as the basis for claiming an equitable interest in the family home under a constructive trust, is materially different from that of a contributor whose claim is founded on a resulting trust.

In the case of a resulting trust, the equitable interest of the contributor is determined exclusively by reference to the size of his contribution. By contrast, the Court of Appeal has held in *Midland Bank v Cooke* (1995) that where a spouse (or co-habitee), who is claiming an equitable interest in the family home under a constructive trust, establishes that she made direct contributions, the court will assess the size of her beneficial entitlement by undertaking a survey of the whole course of dealings between both partners relating to their ownership and occupation of the property; their sharing of the advantages and disadvantages associated with the property and their general conduct. If such a wide ranging survey discloses an intention on their part that the equitable interest in the property was to be shared in proportions different from their respective contributions, the court would give effect to this intention.

(2) *Detrimental reliance:* once the common intention is present, the detrimental reliance may assume various forms. These include:

- contributing to the purchase price or mortgage repayments (*per* Lord Bridge in *Lloyd's Bank v Rosset*);

- contributing towards household expenses: see *Grant v Edwards*;

- supporting the other partner's business ventures which are financed by loans secured by the family home: see *Hammond v Mitchell*;

- contributing financially towards the cost of conversion works on the property: see *Drake v Whipp* (1995);

- contributing in kind to improving the property: see *Eves v Eves*.

By contrast, where the contribution consists of the performance of routine domestic chores (for example, cooking, child-raising, weekend do-it-yourself activities, etc) a constructive trust will not be imposed on this account: see *Burns* and *Midland Bank v Dobson*.

4   Charitable trusts

Philanthropic persons often seek to contribute to the well being of society either:

- by making donations to voluntary bodies established for charitable purposes; or

- by giving property or money to trustees of their own choice to be held for purposes which are charitable.

The significance of charitable status

The Charity Commissioners and courts often have to determine whether a trust or voluntary body is charitable. Where a trust is recognised as charitable, it enjoys certain advantages which do not extend to trusts in the private domain. In particular:

- a private trust fails if its objects are uncertain, whereas a trust which is recognised as charitable is valid even if it does not specify a precise purpose;

- a private trust will also fail where the settlor's intention cannot be carried out but a charitable trust is much less likely to fail on this account in view of the *cy-près* doctrine;

- the perpetuity rules do not apply with the same degree of stringency to charitable trusts as they do to private trusts;

- charitable trusts enjoy many fiscal advantages over private trusts (for example, exemptions from income/corporation/capital gains tax, VAT, stamp duties and relief from non-domestic rates).

Essential requirements of a valid charitable trust

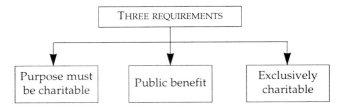

THREE REQUIREMENTS

Purpose must be charitable | Public benefit | Exclusively charitable

The requirement that the purpose must be charitable

In its popular sense, charity is associated with the notion of benevolence towards one's fellow men. In the legal sphere, the concept of charity has acquired a technical meaning which does not always correspond with its ordinary usage.

The preamble to the Charitable Uses Act (CUA) 1601

For a trust to be charitable in the legal sense, its purpose(s) must either:

- fall within the range of purposes expressly enumerated in the preamble to the CUA; or

- be sufficiently analogous to the purposes enumerated in the preamble to be deemed to come 'within the spirit and intendment of the CUA': see, in particular, *Morice v Bishop of Durham* (1805) and *Scottish Burial Reform Society v Glasgow Corporation* (1968).

The fact that the preamble to such an antiquated statute should continue to form the basis for determining charitable status has attracted some criticism and has prompted suggestions that a more modern legislative definition or list of charitable purposes ought to be devised. Significantly, however, the government White Paper on *Charities: A Framework for the Future* (1989) opposed such legislative intervention on the grounds that:

(a) it would hinder the flexibility and scope for development of charitable purposes;

(b) it might lead to certain long established charitable purposes becoming non-charitable;

(c) any list would soon become the subject of judicial pronouncements thus making the new law as complex as the existing law.

This stance is reflected in the Charities Act 1993, which was enacted in response to the White Paper and which contains no all-embracing definition or comprehensive list of modern-day charitable purposes. This means, in effect, that in English law the preamble remains the primary frame of reference for the conferment of charitable status. This has recently been confirmed by the Charity Commission in its Framework Document on the Review of the Register of Charities (1998), although the Commission has, at the same time, sought to make the preamble more relevant to the present day by identifying certain characteristics to be taken into account when dealing with an application for charitable status.

The 'Pemsel' classification of charitable purposes

In the light of the purposes specified in the preamble and those purposes adjudged to be within its spirit and intendment, Lord McNaghten stated in *CIT v Pemsel* (1891) that charitable purposes fell into four broad categories or 'principal divisions'.

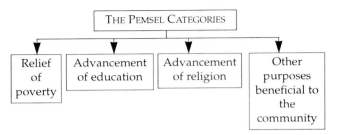

THE PEMSEL CATEGORIES

| Relief of poverty | Advancement of education | Advancement of religion | Other purposes beneficial to the community |

(1) The relief of poverty

The purposes in the CUA include 'the relief of aged, impotent and *poor* people'. This has been construed disjunctively to mean that a trust is charitable if its beneficiaries are poor without being old or infirm: see *Rowntrees Housing Association v AG* (1983).

Poverty, as Evershed MR pointed out in *Re Coulthurst* (1951), is a word of wide and indefinite import. It may range from outright destitution to the relative deprivation of a person who has known better times. As a general guide, he suggests that a person can fairly be regarded as poor if he has to go short in the ordinary acceptance of the word, regard being had to his status in life and so forth.

The clearest indication that the intended purpose is to relieve poverty is where the declaration of trust explicitly refers to poverty or similar words: see, for example, 'needy': *Re Reed* (1893); *Re Scarisbrick* (1951); 'indigent': *Weir v Crum-Brown* (1908); 'limited means': *Re Gardom* (1914); 'fall[en] on evil days': *Re Young's WT* (1951).

Even where such explicit words are not used, the very nature of a gift may denote that it is intended to relieve poverty: see, for example, *Biscoe v Jackson* (1887) (establishment of soup kitchen); *Re Lucas* (1922) (modest weekly payments to the old). A trust will not, however, qualify as one for the relief of poverty where its benefits are not exclusively reserved for the poor, even if it is framed in terms which suggest that those who are likely to claim the benefits will be poor: see *Re Gwyon* (1930) and *Re Sander's WT* (1954), but contrast the latter case with *Re Niyazi's WT* (1978).

(2) The advancement of education

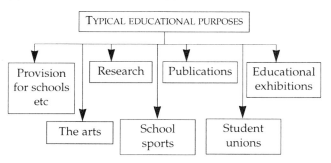

The preamble mentions 'the education ... of orphans' as well as 'the maintenance of schools of learning, free schools and scholars in universities'. The ancient universities and public schools have long enjoyed charitable status which has now been extended to newer universities, colleges and schools: see, for example, *AG v Margaret and Regius Professors in Cambridge* (1682); *The Case of Christ's College Cambridge* (1757); and *Re Mariette* (1915).

The advancement of education is not restricted to the process of formal learning in a classroom environment. It encompasses a wide range of other activities which in the words of *ICLR v AG* (1972) contribute to 'the improvement of a useful branch of human knowledge and its public dissemination'.

The following have been held to be charitable under this head:

Research:	Contrast the position of Harman J in *Re Shaw's WT* (1957) with that of Wilberforce J in *Re Hopkin's WT* (1964). *Note*, also, the conditions laid down by Slade J in *McGovern v AG* (1981)
Educational publications:	*ICLR v AG* (Law Reports); *Re Stanford* (1924) (New English dictionary)
Educational exhibitions:	*British Museum Trustees v White* (1826); *Re Lopes* (1931)
Artistic activities:	*Re Shakespeare Memorial Trust* (1923); *Re Delius* (1957); *Royal Choral Society v IRC* (1943). Contrast with *Re Pinion* (1965) where charitable status was refused
Sports in education:	*Re Mariette* (1915); *Re Dupree's DT* (1945) and *IRC v McMullen* (1981). *Note*, however, Vaisey J's remarks in *Dupree* concerning the difficulties in deciding which sports are educational and which are not
Students unions:	To the extent that they promote the general welfare of members and cater for their social, physical and cultural needs, the law treats the unions as charitable: see *Baldry v Feintuck* (1972); *London Hospital Medical College v IRC* (1976); *AG v Ross* (1986); *Webb v O'Doherty* (1991)

Politics masquerading as education: Cases such as *Re Bushnell* (1975), *McGovern v AG* and *Southwood v AG* (1998) have established that a trust or organisation whose purposes are ostensibly educational will not be accorded charitable status where these purposes are meant to further some political agenda, ideology or goal. By the same token, cases such as *Baldry v Feintuck* and *AG v Ross* have held that bodies which are considered to be charitable in the educational sphere will be precluded from engaging in political activities or supporting political causes. See, further, the Charity Commission Guidelines on Political Activities and Campaigning by Charities (1994, 1995).

(3) The advancement of religion

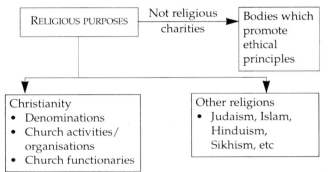

Christianity: The charitable purposes enumerated in the CUA include the repair of churches. In the centuries which have followed, numerous other purposes and organisations associated with Christianity have been recognised as charitable. In the first place, charitable status has been conferred on various Christian denominations and movements: see, for example:

• *Re Barnes* (1930); *Re Tonbridge School Chapel (No 2)* (1993)	Church of England
• *Re Schoales* (1930); *Re Flinn* (1948); *Re Hetherington* (1989)	Roman Catholic Church
• *Re Strickland's WT* (1936)	Baptist Church
• *Re Nesbitt's WT* (1953)	Unitarians
• *Holmes v AG* (1981)	Plymouth Brethren
• *Re Fowler* (1914)	Salvation Army
• *Thornton v Howe* (1862); *Re Watson* (1973); and *Funnell v Stewart* (1996)	Obscure sects on the fringes of Christianity

Furthermore, gifts for a wide range of purposes connected with Christianity have also been held to be charitable including:

• Maintenance of the fabric of a church or chapel	*Re King* (1923) stained glass window; *Re Pardoe* (1906) church bells; *AG v Oakover* (1736) church organ; *AG v Day* (1900) the gallery; *Re Eighmie* (1935) church cemetery
• Upkeep of the clergy	*Pember v Inhabitants of Kington* (1639); *Middleton v Clitheroe* (1798); *Re Williams* (1927); *Re Forster* (1939)
• Preaching of sermons	*Re Parker's Charity* (1863)
• The saying of masses	*Re Caus* (1934); *Re Hetherington*
• Promoting missionary work abroad	*Re Maguire* (1870); *Re Clergy Society* (1856)

• Choral singing in church	*Re Royce* (1940)
• Prizes for Sunday school	*Re Strickland*
• Gifts to religious communities	*Re Banfield* (1968) (except cloistered communities: see *Gilmour v Coats* (1949))

Other ways in which a donor may denote that a gift is meant to promote Christianity are:

• by stating that it should be applied 'for God's work' (*Re Barker's WT* (1948)) or 'to the service of God' (*Re Darling* (1896)) or using other words to the same effect;

• by making the gift to a clergyman (for example, a Bishop or vicar) in terms which limit the scope of the gift to the donee's religious functions: see *Re Garrard* (1907); *Re Flinn* (1948); *Re Rumball* (1956); *Re Bain* (1930); *Re Simson* (1946); and *Re Eastes* (1948).

Contrast with other cases like *Farley v Westminster Bank* (1939) and *Dunne v Byrne* (1912) which involved gifts to clergymen for purposes that went beyond religion.

The charitable status of non-Christian faiths: In *Thornton v Howe*, Romilly MR observed that the court 'makes no distinction between one sort of religion and another'. This view was echoed in *Neville Estates v Madden* (1962) by Cross J who affirmed that, 'as between religions, the law stands neutral, but it assumes that any religion is better than no religion at all'. He therefore held that a trust for the purpose of building and running a synagogue was a valid trust for the advancement of religion. By the same token, the charitable status of a mosque was judicially recognised in *Birmingham Mosque Trust v Alavi* (1992). More recently, the charitable status of an Hindu sect was upheld in *Varsani v Jesani* (1998).

At the same time, the Charity Commissioners have registered as charitable, various organisations which propagate non-Christian faiths such as Islam, Hinduism and Sikhism.

The status of non-religious bodies which promote ethical principles: It emerges from cases like *Re South Place Ethical Society* (1980) and *United Grand Lodge v Holborn LBC* (1957) that such bodies are not considered to be charitable in the religious sphere, though they might be charitable within another sphere.

(4) Other purposes beneficial to the community

This residual category reflects the fact that some purposes which the CUA identifies as charitable are not directly connected with poverty, education or religion but are nevertheless of benefit to society; for example, the relief of the aged and impotent or the repair of bridges, highways, etc. Numerous other purposes not expressly referred to in the Act have also been held to come within this residual category. In *Williams Trustees v IRC* (1947), Lord Simmonds stated that, in order for such a purpose to be charitable under this head, it must not only benefit the community but must do so in a manner that is within the spirit and intendment of the CUA. A different approach was adopted by Russell LJ in *ICLR v AG* (1971) where he suggested that any purpose which was demonstrably beneficial to the community ought to be charitable under this head unless there was some good reason for holding otherwise.

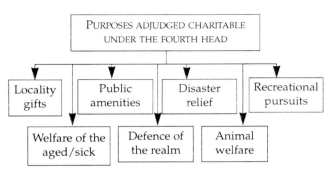

The following have been held to be charitable under the fourth head:

• Gifts for the inhabitants of a locality	*Goodman v Saltash* (1882); *Peggs v Lamb* (1993)
• The welfare of the elderly	*Re Lucas* (1922); *Re Bradbury* (1950); *Re Glyn's WT* (1950); *Re Robinson* (1951); *Re Cottam* (1955); *Rowntree MT Housing Association v AG* (1983)
• Relief of sickness	– Hospitals: *Re Smith's WT* (1962); *Re Resch's WT* (1969) – Home for nurses in a hospital: *Re White's WT* (1951) – Training of nurses: *RCN v St Marylebone Corpn* (1959) – Medical research: *Steel v Wellcome Custodian Trustees* (1988) – Accommodation for patient's relatives: *Re Dean's WT* (1950)

		– Relieving physical or psychological illness or addictions: *Re Lewis* (1955); *Re Chaplin* (1933); and *Re Banfield* (1968)
• Provision and maintenance of public works/amenities		*AG v Governors of Harrow School* (1754); *Jones v Williams* (1767); *Forbes v Forbes* (1854); *Re Spence* (1939)
• Relief of human suffering and distress		– Disaster appeals enjoy charitable status provided the terms of the appeal are exclusively charitable: see *Re North Devon, etc, Relief Fund Trusts* (1953). Contrast with *Re Gillingham Bus DF* (1958)
		– Charitable status is also enjoyed by the emergency services and search and rescue organisations: *Re Wokingham Fire Brigade Trusts* (1951); *Thomas v Howell* (1874)
• Defence of the realm		– Protection from air attacks: *Re Driffil* (1949)
		– Improving military marksmanship: *Re Stephens* (1892)
		– Gift to officers' mess: *Re Good* (1905)
		– Promotion of sports in an army regiment: *Re Gray* (1925)

• The welfare of animals	Upheld as charitable: *University of London v Yarrow* (1857); *Re Wedgewood* (1915); *Re Moss* (1949). But, animal protection which does not serve man's interests is not charitable: *Re Grove-Grady* (1929) and *National Anti-Vivisection Soc v IRC* (1948)
• Recreation/sports	– Sports/recreational activities are not in themselves charitable: see *Re Nottage* (1895); *Re Patten* (1929); *IRC v City Of Glasgow Police AA* (1953); *Williams' Trustees v IRC* (1947); *IRC v Baddeley* (1955) – Provision of recreational amenities and promotion of sports are charitable in the following contexts: • where the intended participants are pupils/ students (*Re Marriette*; *Re Dupree's DT*; *IRC v McMullen*); or in the armed forces (*Re Gray*) • where the amenities are open to the public or the inhabitants of a locality: *Re Hadden* (1932); *Re Morgan* (1955); *Guild v IRC* (1992); *Oldham BC v AG* (1993)

- where the amenities serve 'the interests of social welfare' as defined in the Recreational Charities Act (1958): see *Wynn v Skegness UDC* (1966); *IRC v McMullen*; *Guild v IRC*

The public benefit requirement

As Farwell J observed in *Re Delany* (1902), 'charity is necessarily altruistic and involves the idea of benefit to others'. This notion of altruism is reflected in the general rule that a trust is not charitable if its intended beneficiaries are those for whom the donor would feel naturally obliged to provide; whereas it will be charitable if it is intended to benefit the wider community or the public at large in some way.

This rule has assumed particular importance in modern times, when many settlors seek to alleviate the heavy burden of personal and corporate taxation by 'enlist[ing] the assistance of the law of charity in private endeavours in order to gain tax benefits', *per* Lord Cross in *Dingle v Turner* (1972).

The degree of strictness with which this rule applies depends on which of Lord McNaghten's four headings is in issue:

Poverty

A gift to specified individuals who happen to be poor will not be deemed to be charitable however numerous they may be. By contrast, the courts have accepted in a long line of cases that a gift which is exclusively for the benefit of the poor members of a designated class is charitable, even if the class is small and a close personal nexus exists between the donor and its members:

Designated class	Relevant cases
• Donor's relations	Isaac v Defriez (1754); Re Scarisbrick's WT (1951); Re Cohen (1973); Re Segelman (1995)
• Poor employees	Re Gosling (1900); Gibson v South American Stores (1950); Dingle v Turner (1972)
• Members of a common trade or profession	Thompson v Thompson (1844) writers; Spiller v Maude (1881) actors
• Members of friendly society	Re Buck (1896)
• Members of donor's club	Re Young (1951)

In the light of these cases, Hanbury and Martin have concluded that 'the requirement of public benefit has been reduced in the field of poverty almost to vanishing point'.

Education
The public benefit requirement is more stringently applied in the educational sphere than it is in the field of poverty.

Where the benefits of an educational trust are available not to the public at large but only to the members of a specified class, it will be charitable only if the class forms an appreciable section of the community. According to the test laid down in *Re Compton* (1945), this will be the case if two criteria are met:

- the members of the class must not be numerically negligible; and

- the quality which distinguishes the members of the class from the community at large must not be one which depends on their relationship to a particular individual.

Applying this test, the court held that a trust to educate the descendants of three named persons was not charitable.

Subsequently, in *Oppenheim v Tobacco Securities Trust* (1951), the House of Lords invoked the *Oppenheim* test as the basis for holding that a trust for the education of the children of employees and former employees of a tobacco company was not charitable. *Note*, however, the dissenting judgment of Lord MacDermott who drew attention to the difficulties and contradictions which are liable to arise if the test is taken to its logical conclusion. See, also, the judgment of Lord Cross in *Dingle v Turner*.

Employers have sometimes attempted to avoid the implications of the *Compton* test by creating educational trusts ostensibly for the general public while prevailing on the trustees to utilise the bulk of the trust fund to educate the children of employees. A trust of this nature was recognised as charitable in *Re Koettgen* (1954). By contrast, a similar type of scheme was denied charitable status in *IRC v Educational Grants Association* (1967): see, also, *Caffor v Income Tax Commissioner Colombo* (1961).

Religion

The operation of the public benefit requirement in the religious sphere is most vividly illustrated by *Gilmour v Coats* where a gift to an order of cloistered nuns, who had no contact with the outside world, was held not to be charitable.

The position is different where the gift is to a religious body or movement which does not restrict its services or observances to a closed group of members. It has been held, in cases like *Thornton v Howe* (1862), *Re Watson* (1973) and *Re Le Cren Clarke* (1995), that such a gift fulfils the public benefit requirement even where the body or movement is an obscure one with very few adherents.

Other purposes beneficial to the community

The public benefit requirement is central to the validity of trusts which come within the fourth heading. According to *Verge v Somerville* (1924), the charitable status of such trusts depends on whether the benefits which they provide are available to the community at large or an appreciable section of the community.

The courts have pronounced on the operation of the public benefit requirement under the fourth heading in cases such as:

- *Williams Trustees v IRC* (1947): where it was held that a trust for the benefit of Welsh people in London was not charitable since they did not form an appreciable section of the community; and

- *IRC v Baddeley* (1955): where it was held that a trust which provided a recreational outlet for members/would-be members of the Methodist church in West Ham (among other things) was not charitable since this was not a section of the community but a class within a class.

Although cases like *Goodman v Saltash* and *Peggs v Lamb* have concluded that trusts for the inhabitants of a defined geographical area are charitable, it has been observed by Lord Cross in *Dingle v Turner* that the operation of the public benefit requirement may be problematic where such trusts are concerned, for example, a trust for the ratepayers of the Royal Borough of Kensington may be seen from one perspective as a charitable trust for a section of the community and from another perspective as trust for a fluctuating body of private individuals.

Finally, as Lord Simmonds emphasised in *Baddely,* once the benefits of a trust are open to the public or an appreciable section thereof, the trust is deemed to be charitable even if relatively few people take advantage of the benefits. Thus, for instance: 'A bridge which is available for all the public may undoubtedly be a charity and it is indifferent how many people use it.'

The requirement that the trust must be exclusively charitable

A trust which is framed in terms which enable the trustees without being in breach of trust to expend any part of the trust fund on non-charitable purposes is liable to fail on the ground that it is not exclusively charitable. In *Williams Trustees v IRC*, for instance, a trust which was predominantly for valid educational purposes was held not to be exclusively charitable because one of its purposes (that is, promotion of sport and recreation among Welsh people living in London) was not deemed to be charitable: see also *IRC v City of Glasgow Police AA* (1953).

The failure of a charitable trust on this ground is often the result of imprecise drafting. The major difficulty in this regard is the inappropriate use of words like benevolent, deserving, philanthropic, public and worthy which have the same connotation as the concept of charity in ordinary usage but which are considered to be of wider import than charity in the legal sense. Cases such as *Morice v Bishop of Durham* (1805) and *Re Gillingham Bus DF* (1958) have held that the effect of using such words is that the trust will not be exclusively charitable.

The problem is especially acute where the draftsman uses the word charitable in combination with such words of wider import. The guiding principles in such cases may be summarised as follows:

- Where the connecting word is '**or**', this is ordinarily construed disjunctively which means that the trust will not be regarded as exclusively charitable: see, for example, *Blair v Duncan* (1902) (charitable or public); *Re Diplock* (1948) (charitable or benevolent); *AG v National Provincial Bank* (1924) (charitable or patriotic); and *Houston v Burns* (1918) (public, benevolent or charitable). But, note *Re Bennet* (1920) where a gift 'to charity or other public purpose' was held to be exclusively charitable.

- Where the connecting word is '**and**', this is ordinarily construed conjunctively so that the word of wider import is drawn into the orbit of the charitable and the trust is, in effect, exclusively charitable: see *Blair v Duncan* (charitable and public); *Re Sutton* (1885) (charitable and deserving); and *Re Best* (1904) (charitable and benevolent).

The requirement that a trust must be exclusively charitable has been relaxed in the following contexts:

- where the inclusion of a non-charitable element is designed to facilitate the performance of the trust's charitable purpose: see *Re Coxen* (1948);

- where the non-charitable element is merely incidental to the charitable purpose which constitutes the basis of the trust: see *IRC v City of Glasgow Police AA*; *ICLR v AG*; and *Re Le Cren Clarke*;

- where the trust is framed in terms which enable the court to sever the part of the trust fund intended for charity from the part intended for non-charitable purposes: see *Salusbury v Denton* (1857); and

- by virtue of the Charitable Trusts (Validation) Act 1954, where a trust is declared for purposes which are partly charitable and partly non-charitable and the instrument creating the trust came into effect before 16 December 1952, the trust will operate as if it were exclusively for the charitable purposes: see *Re Wyke's WT* (1961); *Re Meade's Trust Deed* (1961); and *Leahy v AG New South Wales* (1959).

The *cy-près* doctrine

Where a charitable trust is validly declared, circumstances may render it impossible, impracticable or inappropriate to carry out the donor's charitable purpose. In such an event, it is often possible to give effect to the donor's charitable intention by applying the *cy-près* doctrine. The effect of the doctrine is to enable the trust property to be used for some other purpose which resembles the donor's original purpose.

It is a different matter where a trust fails because it does not satisfy any of the requirements for a valid charitable trust. In such a case, the defect cannot be cured by invoking the *cy-près* doctrine. The doctrine was not relied on, for instance, in *Re Gillingham Bus DF* and *Re Jenkin's WT* (1966), both of which involved trusts whose purposes were not exclusively charitable.

Operation of the doctrine before 1960

Before the Charities Act 1960 was enacted, the doctrine applied:

- *where there was a surplus after a specified charitable purpose had been duly accomplished*: see, for example, *Re King* (1923) where a testator left £1,500 to install a stained glass window in a church. The cost of the window was about £800 and it was held that the balance should be spent on a second window; and

- *where it was impossible/impracticable to perform the specified purpose*: in *Biscoe v Jackson* (1887), for instance, there was a legacy of £4,000 to provide a soup kitchen and cottage hospital in Shoreditch. When this proved to be impossible because there was no suitable land in the area, it was held that the fund could be applied *cy-près* to other purposes: see, also, *Re Burton's Charity* (1938); *Re Dominion Student's Hall Trust* (1947); and *Re Hillier* (1944).

The doctrine was, however, inapplicable where the intended purpose did not represent an efficient use of resources or was outdated or difficult to fulfil or otherwise unsuitable, without being impossible or impracticable. A case in point is *Re Weir's Hospital* (1910) where property which a testator had devised to be used as a hospital was unsuited for this purpose but the court refused to permit the property to be applied *cy-près* to some other purpose.

Operation of the doctrine since 1960

The 1960 Act (which has now been superseded by the Charities Act 1993) extended the doctrine to a variety of circumstances which do not necessarily entail impossibility or impracticability. It is provided in s 13 that the original purposes of a charitable gift can be altered to allow the property or part of it to be applied *cy-près*, in the following circumstances:

- where the original purpose has as far as possible been fulfilled;

- where the original purpose cannot be carried out at all or carried out as directed or according to the spirit of the gift;

- where the original purpose utilises only part of the property;

- where the property and other property applicable for similar purposes can be more effectively pooled together and suitably applied towards common purposes;

- where the gift was made by reference to a geographical area which has since ceased to be a unit or to a class of persons or area which has since ceased to be suitable or practicable: see *Peggs v Lamb* (1993); and

- where the original purpose has since it was laid down:

    כ been adequately provided for by other means;

   כ ceased to be charitable in law; or

   כ ceased to provide a suitable and effective method of using the property regard being had to the spirit of the gift. See *Re Lepton's Charity* (1972) and *Varsani v Jesani*.

Initial failure and the requirement of general charitable intent

The courts have established in a long line of cases that, where a charitable gift cannot take effect at the outset due to the *initial failure* of the donor's charitable purpose, the doctrine will only apply if the donor possessed *a general charitable intent*.

Such intent was discernible for instance in *Biscoe v Jackson* where the sum of £4,000, which a testator directed was to be used to set up a soup kitchen/hospital, was to be taken out of a bequest of £10,000 which he had expressly made to charity: see, also, *Re Lysaght* (1966) and *Re Woodhams* (1981).

By contrast, the *cy-près* doctrine is excluded in cases of initial failure, where the donor did not evince a general charitable intent, but rather intended that the gift should be used for the purpose prescribed by him and nothing else. Thus, in *Re White's Trust* (1886), a gift to establish an almshouse for poor tinplate workers failed because no suitable site was available and the fund was insufficient to maintain an almshouse. The *cy-près* doctrine was held to be inapplicable on the ground that the donor did not intend the gift to be used for any other purpose and a resulting trust arose in favour of the donor's estate: see, also, *Re Rymer* (1905); *Re Wilson* (1913) and *Re Good's WT* (1950).

Gifts to charities which have ceased to exist
Where property is given to a charity which has become defunct at the date of the gift, this will ordinarily be treated as a case of initial failure and the *cy-près* doctrine will apply only if the donor had a general charitable intent.

In two contexts, however, a gift to a defunct charity will not give rise to initial failure (and will therefore be valid without the need to prove a general charitable intention). These are:

- Where the relevant charity though no longer in being is deemed to exist in a different form at the date of the gift (for example, by having been amalgamated with other similar charities into a larger entity) as happened in *Re Faraker* (1912). But, note *Re Stemson's WT* (1970) which signifies that the dissolution of an *incorporated charity* and transfer of its assets to another body will not be treated as existence in a different form.

• Where the gift is construed not as a gift to the defunct charity as such but as a gift for its purposes and such purposes are capable of being fulfiled by other means.

The following points should be noted in this connection:

(a) The courts are most inclined to adopt this construction whee there is a testamentary gift to an *unincorporated charity* by name with nothing more and the charity has ceased to exist at the testator's death. See *Re Vernon's WT* (1972); and *Re Finger's WT* (1972).

(b) Where the gift is to an *incorporated charity* which has ceased to exist at the testator's death, it emerges from *Re Finger* that it will not ordinarily be construed as a gift for its purposes. It will accordingly fail unless the court can discern a general charitable intention which will enable it to invoke the *cy-près* doctrine.

(c) Where the gift is to an incorporated charity which the court had ordered to be wound up but which had not yet been dissolved at the testator's death, the gift will not fail so as to invoke the *cy-près* doctrine. Rather it will be treated as part of the charity's assets available on its eventual dissolution for distribution among its creditors. See *Re ARMS Ltd* (1997).

Gifts to charities which have never existed
Where a gift is made to a charity which has never existed at all, this will result in initial failure. It follows that the *cy-près* doctrine will apply only if the donor had a general charitable intent. However, it appears from *Re Harwood*

(1936) that the courts are more inclined to ascribe a general charitable intention to the donor in the case of a gift to a charity which never existed than in the case of one which once existed but became defunct.

Combined gifts to charitable and non-charitable bodies

A donor may direct that certain property should be divided among several named bodies. Where it happens that all these bodies are charities, except for one, the gift to the non-charitable body almost invariably fails, as happened in *Re Satterthwaite's WT* (1966) and *Re Jenkins WT*.

An issue which arises in such cases is whether the fact that the gifts are predominantly in favour of charities is indicative of a general charitable intention on the donor's part. Judicial opinion is divided on the matter. Such an intention was held to exist in *Satterthwaite* and the court accordingly directed that the gift to the non-charitable body should be applied *cy-près* towards charitable purposes.

By contrast, in *Jenkins,* the court refused to infer such an intention from the fact that all but one of the intended donees was charitable and concluded that there was no basis for applying the *cy-près* doctrine to the share of the non-charitable body.

The position with regard to public contributions

Where funds have been raised from the public for a charitable purpose which fails, s 14 of the Charities Act 1993 provides that:

- any contributor who either executes a disclaimer or does not come forward to reclaim his contribution after prescribed advertisements and inquiries have been made loses his entitlement and his contribution will be applied *cy-près;*

- if funds have been raised in a manner not adapted for distinguishing one contribution from another (for example, collection boxes) or represent the proceeds of lotteries or similar activities, no advertisements or inquiries are required before such funds can be applied *cy-près*.

Subsequent failure

The *cy-près* doctrine also comes into play in the event of the failure of a charitable gift after it has actually taken effect. Such subsequent failure may occur, for instance:

- where property is given to a charity which was in existence when the gift was made but which has since ceased to exist;

- where a gift is made to trustees for a charitable purpose which is carried on for some time but is then discontinued because it has become impossible or impracticable to sustain or is no longer considered suitable;

- where a gift is made to trustees for a charitable purpose which is duly completed leaving a surplus (as happened in *Re King*).

In the event of subsequent failure, because the property affected is already in the charitable domain, the *cy-près* doctrine applies without any need to prove that the donor had a general charitable intention. This was made abundantly clear in *Re Slevin* (1891) where T left a legacy for an orphanage. This orphanage existed at T's death but was shut before T's will was administered. The court held that the gift would be applied *cy-près* without regard to T's charitable intent since this was a case of subsequent failure in that the orphanage was still in existence at the time the gift: see, also, *Re Wright* (1954) and *Re Moon* (1948).

Overview of the cy-près doctrine

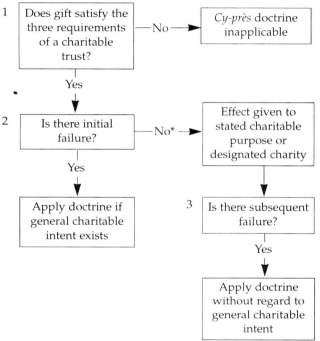

* *Note*: there will be no initial failure where:
  * the specified charitable purpose is capable of being fulfilled;

- the designated charity exists at date of gift;
- the designated charity exists in a different form at date of gift;
- the gift is to a defunct charity for its purposes which are attainable by other means.

5 The administration of trusts

Appointment, retirement and removal of trustees

Appointment of trustees

Capacity

As a general rule, any human being or corporate body with the capacity to own property may be appointed a trustee.

The appointment of infants as trustees is specifically prohibited by s 20 of the LPA (though infants have been held to be trustees under resulting trusts in *Re Vinogradoff* (1935) and *Re Muller* (1953)).

Number of trustees

It is open to a settlor to specify a minimum or maximum number of trustees in the trust instrument. Where a minimum of two trustees is prescribed, a trust corporation may administer the trust as sole trustee. See *Re Duxbury's ST* (1993).

Where the trust instrument is silent, there is no upper or lower limit on the number of trustees a settlor/testator may appoint. However, it is inadvisable to appoint only one or to appoint too many.

Where the trust relates to real property, there is no strict lower limit but at least two trustees are usually appointed since a sole trustee of land cannot give a valid receipt to a purchaser if it is sold. An upper limit of four is imposed by s 34(2) of the TA, but this limit is dispensed with where the land is held on trust for charitable, ecclesiastical or public purposes.

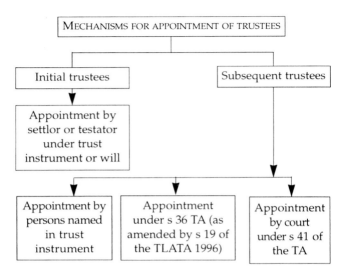

Appointment of the initial trustees

In the case of *inter vivos* trusts, the trustees are usually named in the trust instrument by the settlor (who may himself be one of the trustees); while in the case of testamentary trusts, the trustees are usually named by the testator in his will.

It sometimes happens that there are no initial trustees available to administer a trust at its inception. In such an event, the operative principle is expressed in the equitable maxim that 'a trust will not fail for want of trustees'.

In line with this principle, the courts have been prepared to give effect to testamentary trusts where no trustee was named in the will or all the trustees so named died before the testator or disclaimed the trust. See, for example, *Re Smirthwaite* (1871) and *Dodkin v Brunt* (1868).

By the same token, it has been held that, where a settlor has executed an *inter vivos* transfer or conveyance to trustees then living, the trust will not fail if the trustees all later die or disclaim the property. See, for example, *Jones v Jones* (1874) and *Mallott v Wilson* (1903).

Appointment of subsequent trustees

The need may arise from time to time to appoint new trustees *in place of* or *in addition to* the initial trustees. This can be done by inserting an express power of appointment in the trust instrument in favour of the settlor or in favour of some other person.

Section 36 of the TA: Considerable scope also exists for the appointment of replacement and additional trustees under s 36 of the TA.

Replacement trustees: Under s 36(1) and (2), one or more new trustees may be appointed in place of a trustee who:

- is dead;

- remains outside the UK for a continuous period of 12 months;

- desires to be discharged from the trust or refuses to act or is unfit to act (for example, due to bankruptcy or criminal dishonesty);

- is incapable of acting (for example, due to old age or mental disorder) or is an infant; or

- has been removed from the trust in the exercise of a power contained in the trust instrument.

The power of appointing replacement trustees lies with:

- any person nominated in the trust instrument for this purpose;

- the surviving or continuing trustee(s) for the time being; or

- the personal representatives of the last surviving/ continuing trustee (in that order).

In cases where an appointment is to be made by surviving or continuing trustees, *Re Coates to Parsons* (1886) and *Re Stoneham's ST* (1953) have decided that the non-participation of the departing trustee in the process will not invalidate the appointment. However, in view of the provision in s 36(8), that a continuing trustee 'includes a refusing or retiring trustee where he is able to act', it is best, for the avoidance of doubt, to involve the departing trustee in making the appointment, wherever possible.

Additional trustees

Limited scope for appointing additional trustees exists under s 36(1) since it allows for a departing trustee to be replaced by one or more trustees.

For the most part, additional trustees are appointed under s 36(6). Appointments can be made under s 36(6) even if no trustee is being replaced, provided there are no more than three trustees administering the trust and the number after appointment will not exceed four. Under s 36(6), such appointments are to be made by the person(s) nominated for this purpose by the trust instrument or, if there is no such person, by the trustee(s) for the time being.

Section 36(6) has recently been amended by the Trustee Delegation Act 1999. This Act enlarges the categories of persons who may appoint additional trustees to include a donee of a power of attorney granted by all the trustees who intends to exercise trust functions relating to land.

Section 41 of the TA empowers the court to appoint trustees in addition to or in place of existing trustees where it is expedient to make an appointment but it is found to be inexpedient, difficult or impracticable to do so under the trust instrument or under s 36.

Examples of situations in which the courts will intervene are:

- where the parties entitled to appoint new trustees are not in a position to do so for reasons such as:

  - infancy: *Re Parsons* (1940)

  - old age/infirmity: *Re Lemann's WT* (1883)

    Re Phelps (1885)

  - wartime disruptions: *Re May's WT* (1941);

- where the last surviving trustee dies intestate and there is no one to administer his estate;

- where all the trustees named in a will pre-decease the testator: see *Re Smirthwaite;*

- where an appointment is delayed unduly because of disagreements between those empowered to appoint new trustees: see *Re Tempest* (1866).

Re Tempest is also notable because it identified the factors that the court would consider in exercising its jurisdiction, namely:

- the wishes of the settlor and the beneficiaries;

- whether the appointee is likely to favour some beneficiaries at the expense of others; and

- whether the appointment is likely to promote or impede the execution of the trust.

Involvement of beneficiaries in appointment of new trustees: Cases like *Re Higginbottom* (1892) and *Re Brockbank* (1948) decided that once the persons invested with the statutory power to appoint new trustees were willing to do so, their choice of trustees could not be overridden by the beneficiaries even if they were all of full age and absolutely entitled to the whole beneficial interest.

The effect of these decisions has now been reversed by the enactment of s 19 of the TLATA 1996. This provides that, where:

- there is no person expressly nominated by the trust instrument for the purpose of appointing new trustees; and

- the beneficiaries are all of full age and capacity and absolutely entitled to the trust property,

these beneficiaries may give written directions to the trustee(s) for the time being to appoint the person(s) specified in such directions as new trustees of the trust.

Accepting or disclaiming the trust: A trustee may signify his acceptance of the trust by deed, by ordinary writing or orally. In addition, acceptance may be implied, where for example:

- a person named as an executor/trustee in a will obtains probate of the will: see *Mucklow v Fuller* (1821) and *Re Sharman's WT* (1942); or

- a person named as a trustee interferes with the trust property in some way: see *James v Frearson* (1842) and *Urch v Walker* (1838).

A trustee may disclaim the trust by turning down his appointment before acceptance. Such a disclaimer may be by deed, in writing or oral; or it may be inferred from the trustee's conduct (for example, where he neglects to assume office, as in *Clout v Frewer* (1924)).

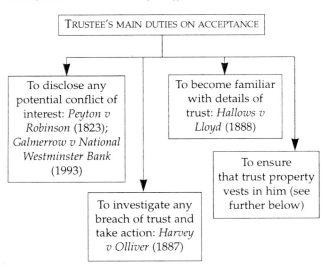

Procedure for vesting

- in the case of an initial trustee, trust property vests in him, where he is named in the trust deed;

- with regard to a subsequent trustee, s 40(1) of the TA provides that once he has been appointed by deed, this automatically vests the property in the new trustee jointly with the existing ones;

- there are, however, certain types of property which do not vest automatically where a new trustee is appointed by deed, notably:
  ○ land mortgaged as security for money owed to the trust;
  ○ land held under a lease, which contains a covenant not to assign without consent;
  ○ stocks and shares.

Retirement of trustees

Retirement in accordance with terms of trust instrument

Judicial discharge in exercise of court's inherent jurisdiction

Retirement under s 36 of the TA where outgoing trustee is to be replaced

Retirement by deed under s 39 of the TA. Only possible if there are at least two remaining trustees or a trust corporation who must consent by *deed* to such retirement

Retirement under s 19 of the TLATA on the written direction of beneficiaries who are all of full age and absolutely entitled to the whole trust property

Removal of trustees

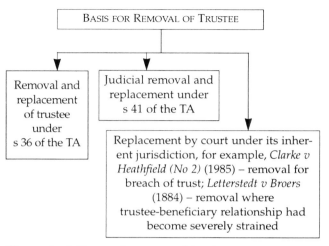

BASIS FOR REMOVAL OF TRUSTEE

Removal and replacement of trustee under s 36 of the TA

Judicial removal and replacement under s 41 of the TA

Replacement by court under its inherent jurisdiction, for example, *Clarke v Heathfield (No 2)* (1985) – removal for breach of trust; *Letterstedt v Broers* (1884) – removal where trustee-beneficiary relationship had become severely strained

The main duties and powers of trustees

The nature of the trustee's responsibilities
The position of the trustee carries such heavy responsibilities that it is 'an act of great kindness in anyone to accept it' – *per* Lord Hardwicke in *Knight v Earl of Plymouth* (1747).

A trustee's basic functions are to perform duties and exercise the powers provided for in the trust instrument as well as general duties and powers prescribed by statute or by the courts.

Duties are obligatory. Accordingly, a beneficiary may proceed against the trustee for breach of trust if he fails to perform a duty. By contrast, the trustee's powers are discretionary, although they are held in a fiduciary capacity and so the trustee must consider periodically whether to exercise them or not. The beneficiary cannot dictate the manner in which the trustee is to exercise his powers: see *Re Beloved Wilkes Charity* (1851); *Re Londonderry's ST* (1965) and *Wilson and Another v The Law Debenture Trust Corp* (1995). Furthermore, the courts will not ordinarily interfere to circumscribe the exercise of a trustee's discretions unless he has acted dishonestly, capriciously, erroneously or without proper judgment: see *Re Manisty's Settlement* (1974) and *Turner v Turner* (1984).

Note, however, that s 11 of the TLATA 1996 contemplates that in the exercise of their powers, trustees of *land* shall:

- so far as practicable consult any beneficiaries who are of full age and beneficially entitled to an interest in possession; and

- so far as consistent with the general interest of the trust, give effect to the wishes of those beneficiaries.

Note, also, that the power to appoint and dismiss trustees collectively exercisable under s 19 of the TLATA by beneficiaries who are of full age and absolutely entitled to trust property now enables such beneficiaries to assert much greater control over the exercise of trustees' powers than had hitherto been the case.

The unanimity rule

Where there are several trustees, each one is required to participate fully in administering the trust. This requirement means that trustees must exercise their powers unanimously unless there is a provision to the contrary in the trust instrument: see *Luke v South Kensington Hotel* (1879); *Re Mayo* (1943); and *Re Butlin's ST* (1976). But, note that the rule does not apply to charitable trusts: see *Perry v Shipway* (1859); and *Re Whitely* (1910).

Remuneration of trustees

Early cases, such as *Robinson v Pett* (1734), established that a trustee was not entitled to payment for administering the trust. More recently, the administration of trusts has become a complex and time consuming business and trustees are now able to charge for their services in a variety of circumstances, notably:

- where the trust instrument contains a charging clause: see *Webb v Earl of Shaftesbury* (1802);

  Note the recommendation of the Law Commission in its 1999 Report on Trustees' Powers and Duties that, in the case of professional trustees, an implied charging clause should be read into the trust instrument unless expressly excluded. This recommendation is reflected in cl 29 of the Draft Trustee Bill accompanying the Report.

- where the court sanctions payment in the exercise of its inherent jurisdiction as in *Re Duke of Norfolk's ST* (1981); *Re Drexel Burnham Lambert* (1994); and *Foster v Spencer* (1995);

- where beneficiaries who are *sui juris* agree to pay the trustee;

- where payment is authorised by statute: for example, s 42 of the TA; s 1(5) of the Judicial Trustees Act 1905; and s 9 of the Public Trustee Act (1906);

- where the trust includes assets in a foreign country and persons administering such assets are paid under the laws of that country: see *Re Northcote's WT* (1949);

- where the trustee is a solicitor and the rule in *Cradock v Piper* (1850) applies.

Note: a trustee will also be repaid for any reasonable expenses he incurs in executing the trust: see s 30(2) of the TA; *Stott v Milne* (1884); and *Hardoon v Belilios* (1901).

The standard of care

The trustees must exercise a high degree of diligence in carrying out the trust. In particular:

- an *unpaid trustee* (for example, the settlor's friend/relation) must in executing the trust take 'all those precautions which an ordinary prudent man of business would take in managing similar affairs of his own', *per* Lord Blackburn in *Speight v Gaunt* (1883);

- Cases such as *Re Waterman's WT* (1952) and *Bartlett v Barclays Bank Trust Co* (1980) as well as the Law Reform Committee's Report on the Powers and Duties of Trustees (1982) signify that a paid trustee is subject to a 'higher standard of diligence and knowledge' or a 'special duty to display expertise' as compared to an unpaid trustee. They do not, however, shed further light on the precise standard demanded of paid trustees.

In its recent Report on the Trustees' Powers and Duties, the Law Commission reaffirmed the general principle that remunerated and professional trustees are expected to demonstrate a higher standard than other trustees and that a trustee who professes to have special expertise beyond that of an ordinary prudent man *is* accountable for any loss incurred by the trust due to his failure to exercise that level of expertise. The Commission recommended that this principle should be given expression in a statutory duty of care. The proposed statutory duty is embodied in cl 1 of the Draft Trustee Bill which provides that a trustee must exercise such care and skill as is reasonable in the circumstances, having regard in particular:

(a) to any special knowledge or expertise that he holds himself out as having; and

(b) if he acts as a trustee in the course of business or a profession, to any special knowledge or expertise that it is reasonable to expect of a person acting in the course of that kind of business or profession.

The trustee's duties

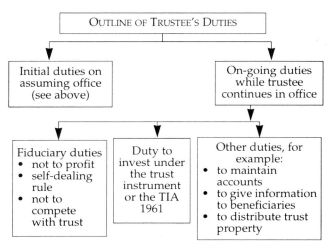

OUTLINE OF TRUSTEE'S DUTIES

Initial duties on assuming office (see above)

On-going duties while trustee continues in office

Fiduciary duties
- not to profit
- self-dealing rule
- not to compete with trust

Duty to invest under the trust instrument or the TIA 1961

Other duties, for example:
- to maintain accounts
- to give information to beneficiaries
- to distribute trust property

Fiduciary duties

These are duties imposed by equity with a view to ensuring that a trustee's interests do not conflict with those of the trust.

(a) Unauthorised profits

As stated in Chapter 3, when dealing with constructive trusts, a trustee or other fiduciary 'is not, unless otherwise expressly provided, entitled to make a profit', *per* Lord Herschell in *Bray v Ford* (1896).

Cases discussed in that chapter, like *Sugden v Crossland* (1876); *Williams v Barton* (1927); *Re Macadam* (1945); *Keech v Sandford* (1726); *Regal (Hastings) v Gulliver* (1942); and *Boardman v Phipps* (1967), establish that a trustee or other fiduciary will be required to hold such profits on constructive trust for their principal.

(b) Purchase of trust property by trustee

Trustees who decide to sell trust property 'have an overriding duty to obtain the best price which they can for their beneficiaries', *per* Wynn-Parry J in *Buttle v Saunders* (1950).

The self-dealing rule: If a trustee is able to purchase trust property he will be tempted not to seek the best possible price. In view of this, equity has evolved the self-dealing rule under which a sale of trust property to a trustee (as well as a sale of a trustee's property to the trust) is voidable by a beneficiary. Four points should be noted regarding the self-dealing rule:

(1) a sale to a trustee may be set aside even if he bought in good faith and at a fair price: see *ex p James* (1803); *ex p Lacey* (1802); *Armitage v Nurse* (1997);

(2) if the arrangement is that trust property will be sold to a trustee after he retires, the sale may also be set aside: see *Wright v Morgan* (1926) unless the sale takes place long after his retirement: see *Re Boles* (1902);

(3) a sale of trust property may be set aside where a trustee is in effect indirectly buying it through another person: see, for example, *Delves v Gray* (1902)) or through a company in which he has a substantial shareholding: see *Re Thompson's Settlement* (1986);

(4) the courts will not set aside a sale on the basis of this rule:

>) where the purchaser is made a trustee after contracting to buy trust property but before completion: see *Re Mulholland's WT* (1949); *Spiro v Glencrown Ltd* (1996);

>) where the purchaser is a bare trustee with no active duties to perform: see *Parkes v White* (1805); and

> ɔ where there are special circumstances which in the court's view make it inappropriate to set aside the sale: see *Clark v Clark* (1884); and *Holder v Holder* (1968).

The fair-dealing rule: the self-dealing rule does not apply where a trustee purchases a beneficiary's interest in trust property (as distinct from purchasing the trust property itself): see *ex p Lacey* (1802).

The operative rule in such cases is the fair-dealing rule under which the beneficiary cannot set aside the sale once the trustee is able to show 'that he has taken no advantage of his position and made full disclosure to the beneficiary and that the transaction was fair and honest', *per* Megarry VC in *Tito v Waddell (No 2)* (1977): see, also, *Coles v Trecothick* (1804); *Thomas v Eastwood* (1877); and *Dougan v MacPherson* (1902).

(c) Competing in business with the trust

A conflict may occur between the duties of a trustee and his personal interest where the trust estate includes a business and the trustee is found to be conducting a business of his own in competition with the trust. Such a conflict arose, for instance, in *Re Thompson* (1930) where the trust estate included a yacht broking business and an injunction was granted to restrain a trustee from embarking on this line of business in the same town.

The duty to invest

As pointed out by the Law Commission in its Report on Trustees' Powers and Duties, 'The administration of most trusts is primarily concerned with the investment of the assets of the trust'. Trustees must always ensure that trust assets are invested properly. Investment encompasses 'the purchase [or retention] of property from which interest or profit is expected', *per* Lawrence J in *Re Wragg* (1919). If property is acquired for another purpose (for example, to accommodate beneficiaries), this does not constitute investment: see *Re Power* (1947).

A well drafted trust instrument often contains an express investment clause. Where the trust instrument is silent or provides for a few investments without expressly confining the trustees to these investments, the Trustee Investments Act (TIA) 1961 sets out a fairly extensive range of investments which trustees are authorised to make.

The Act, however, applies subject to any contrary intention in the trust instrument. Accordingly, its operation will be displaced if the trust instrument requires the trustees to confine their investments to a more restricted range of securities than those set out in the Act. By the same token, where the trust instrument contains a clause empowering the trustees to make investments which go beyond those authorised by the TIA, the trust instrument will prevail. See, for example, *Re Harari's ST* (1949) and *Re Peczenik's ST* (1964).

General principles to be taken into account in making investments

(a) *Trustees must exercise a higher degree of care than in performing other duties*

This is implicit in the remarks of Lord Watson in *Learoyd v Whiteley* (1887) who declared that a trustee must when investing trust assets spurn any investment which is attended with hazard. His duty is not merely:

> ... to take such care only as a prudent man would take if he had only himself to consider. The duty rather is to take such care as an ordinary prudent man would take if he were minded to make an investment for other people for whom he felt morally obliged to provide.

At the same time, Bacon VC has been quick to emphasise in *Re Godfrey* (1883) that no investment can ever be guaranteed to be completely safe since all human affairs carry some degree of risk. This stance is also evident in cases like *Re Chapman* (1896) which held that a trustee who acts honestly and in good faith in making investment decisions, will not be liable for any ensuing loss, simply because the benefit of hindsight shows that he was wrong.

Furthermore, the traditional insistence that trustees should refrain from investments attended by hazard has been tempered by the increasing acceptance of the 'portfolio theory' in the realm of trust investments. In the words of Hoffman J in *Nestlé v National Westminster Bank* (1993), 'modern trustees acting within their investment powers are entitled to be judged by the standards of the current portfolio theory which emphasises the risk of the entire portfolio rather than the risk attaching to each investment taken in isolation'. This suggests in effect that an investment with a potentially high return which on its own may be considered unduly speculative may be justified if it is appropriately balanced by other safer investments within the same portfolio.

(b) *Trustees must diversify their investments*

It is desirable for trustees to diversify their investments so that even if some of them fail to yield dividend others will do so. Section 6(1) of the TIA requires trustees to have regard to the need for such diversification. The Law Commission has stated that this requirement is in conformity with the modern portfolio theory and strongly recommend in its Report on Trustees' Powers and Duties that it should be retained.

(c) *Trustees must maintain a balance between income and capital*

Trustees are bound to act fairly as between different classes of beneficiaries. They must thus select investments which as far as possible yield a reasonable income while preserving the capital value of the trust assets.

It is inappropriate, for example, for trustees to invest in:

- wasting assets which yield a high income while their capital value steadily depreciates (for example, short leases and copyrights); or

- objects which are likely to appreciate in value over time but which yield little or no income (for example, antiques and paintings).

(d) *Trustees should not ordinarily be guided by non-financial considerations*

Buttle v Saunders held that in selling trust property, a trustee must seek the best financial interests of the beneficiaries without regard to underlying ethical implications. In *Cowan v Scargill* (1985), the same stance was adopted in connection with the trustee's duty to invest.

The extent to which ethical considerations should feature in investment decisions poses particular problems in the case of charitable trustees. In the leading case of *Harries v The Church Commissioners* (1992), the court acknowledged that ethical considerations may be material to the extent that charitable trustees may opt not to invest in a highly profitable sector or venture if the investment:

- conflicts directly with the charity's objects; or

- is liable to alienate potential donors or beneficiaries.

The specific issue which fell to be determined in *Harries* was whether the Church Commissioners as trustees of Church of England assets were required to restrict their investments to those which sought to promote the Christian faith even at the expense of maximising the return on investments. The court held that charitable trustees like other trustees had a duty to maximise their profits and that their investments could only be dictated by ethical considerations to the extent that this did not detract from their duty. The fact that the Commissioners were pursuing an investment policy which excluded investments in armaments, tobacco, gambling, etc, was considered acceptable by the court since there was a sufficiently wide range of alternative investments open to them to ensure profitability.

The mechanism for investment under the TIA
(a) *The authorised investments*
These fall into three categories:

Narrower Range (Pt I): Consists of securities which usually have a lower rate of yield but are relatively secure because they guarantee a fixed rate of income and a capital base which is not prone to fluctuation; for example, Defence Bonds, National Savings Bonds, National Savings Certificates and deposits in the National Savings Bank. No investment advice is required by trustees who seek to invest in Pt I securities.

Narrower Range (Pt II): Consists of various securities which are fixed as to the rate of income but which for the most part are liable to fluctuate in terms of their capital value and carry a higher risk than Pt I investments. Examples include:

- traditional gilt-edged securities issued or guaranteed by the UK and other Governments, local authorities, etc;

- debentures of companies registered in the UK;

- deposits in building societies; and

- mortgages of freeholds/leaseholds with at least 60 years to run.

Such securities are generally more risky than those in Pt I and hence investment advice must be sought before making them.

Wider range (Pt III): These were not recognised as authorised investments before the enactment of the TIA. The most important of these securities are the shares of public limited companies quoted on a recognised United Kingdom Stock Exchange (commonly called equities). The company must have a minimum paid up capital of £1 million and must have paid dividends on all its shares in the five years preceding the investments.

Wider range investments generally yield a higher rate of return than narrower range investments but tend to be more susceptible to fluctuations in the financial markets and are thus relatively insecure. Investment advice must be sought before making them.

Note that the Draft Trustee Bill (1999) annexed to the Law Commission's Report on Trustees' Powers and Duties dispenses with the TIA's distinction between investments requiring advice and those which do not. The Bill provides instead that, before exercising any power of investment, the trustee must obtain and consider proper advice unless he reasonably concludes that, in all the circumstances, it is unnecessary or inappropriate to do so.

(b) *Apportionment*

Trustees may opt to invest only in narrower range securities. Where they propose to make wider range investments, they must first of all apportion the trust assets into a *narrower range part* and a *wider range part*.

As originally enacted, s 2(1) of the TIA required the narrower and wider range parts of the trust fund to be of equal value. However, the Trustee Investment (Division of Trust Fund) Order 1996 made pursuant to s 13 of the TIA now provides that any division of the trust fund must be such that the value of the wider range part shall be three times the value of the narrower range part.

After the trust assets have been so divided, the narrower range part can only be invested in narrower range securities; while the wider range part may be invested exclusively in wider range securities or utilised for both wider range and narrower range investments.

Note that the Draft Trustee Bill does not differentiate between narrower and wider range securities and, if enacted, will relieve trustees of the need to apportion trust funds in this manner.

(c) *Accruals*

After apportionment, additional property may accrue to the trust estate. The position in such cases is that:

- where it accrues to the trust estate as a whole (for example, repayment of a debt to the trust estate after apportionment), it will be apportioned between the narrower and wider range parts. With the coming into effect of the aforementioned Order, this will now be done in the proportion of 3:1;

- where it accrues to the trustee as owner of property already comprised in either part of the trust fund (for example, issue of bonus shares to trustee who invests in the wider range), it will not be apportioned but will remain within the part from which it arose.

(d) *Withdrawals*

After apportionment, the trustees may need to make withdrawals from the trust fund for various purposes (for example, in order to exercise their power of advancement). They may do so from either part without the need for a compensating transfer.

(e) *Special powers and special range investments*

A trust instrument may contain special powers of investment which go beyond those set out in the TIA. Such powers may also be conferred by a court order or under the terms of other statutes.

Where a special power provides for the trustees to hold property (including wider range but not narrower range property) otherwise than in accordance with the provisions of the TIA, such property is known as special range property. Typical examples of special range property include shares in a private company and land.

Where the trust instrument contemplates that the trustees should invest only in special range property, the TIA is inapplicable. But, where they are empowered to invest only part of the trust funds in special range property, they must set apart the portion of the trust fund which is to be utilised for this purpose and divide the balance into a narrower range and a wider range part.

(f) *Review of investments*

Trustees are not only required to seek advice before investing in Pt I or Pt II securities but also to determine at what intervals it is desirable to obtain advice regarding the retention of such securities. Trustees are thus expected to review their investments periodically and, in so doing, to proceed on the basis of proper advice. An instructive case is *Nestlé v National Westminster Bank* (1993) where the bank-trustee failed to conduct regular reviews because a misreading of the investment clause in the trust instrument had led it to assume that its investment options were quite narrow. Having regard to the standards of investment practice during much of the period of the trust's subsistence, the Court of Appeal could find no evidence that the lack of such reviews had led to wrong decisions or appreciably lower returns and held that the trustee was not liable for breach of trust.

Mortgages as investments

One form of investment authorised by the TIA is a loan of trust funds secured by a mortgage of land held by the mortgagor as a freeholder or as a lessee with an unexpired residue of at least 60 years.

It is specifically provided in s 8 of the TA, that a trustee who makes such an investment will not be liable for breach of trust in respect of any loss resulting therefrom, where he:

- obtains a report on the value of the property from a person he reasonably believed to be an independent surveyor or valuer;

- acts on the advice of such a person; and

- lends to the mortgagor a sum not exceeding two-thirds of the value placed on the property in the report.

For example, if T has at his disposal £50,000 worth of trust funds which he proposes to lend to M on the security of M's property Blackacre, but it emerges from the valuer's report that Blackacre is worth only £60,0000, s 8 requires T to limit the sum advanced to £40,000. If T does so and an unforeseen drop in property prices later reduces the value of Blackacre to £30,000, T will not be liable for the £10,000 which is outstanding.

However, if T persists in lending the entire £50,000 to M and the value of Blackacre drops to £30,000, the effect of s 9 of the TA is that T will be liable not for the £20,000 which represents the total loss to the trust, but for £10,000 (that is, the difference between the £50,000 actually lent and the £40,000 which could properly have been lent under s 8).

Investments in land

The purchase of land is not an authorised investment under the TIA. Trustees may, however, invest in land:

- where this is expressly authorised by the trust instrument; or

- where investment in land is provided for by other statutes. For example, s 73(1)(xi) of the SLA and s 28(1) of the LPA authorised the investment of capital monies received on the sale of settled land or land held on trust for sale, in the purchase of freehold land or leasehold land with an unexpired residue of at least 60 years.

With particular reference to trusts for sale, an unresolved issue was whether, in the event of the disposition of the entire land held on trust for sale, the trustee could invest the proceeds of sale in purchasing other land. In *Re Wakeman* (1945), it was held that he could not, but this conclusion was called into question by Cohen LJ in *Re Wellsted's WT* (1949).

The matter has now been settled by the TLATA 1996. Section 6(3) and (4) of the Act empower a trustee of land to purchase a legal estate in any land in England and Wales by way of investment; while s 17(1) makes it clear that a trustee of land in this context includes a trustee of the proceeds of sale of land. Significantly, the Law Commission recommended in its Report on Trustees' Duties and Powers that all trustees should be able to acquire freehold or leasehold land in the UK as an investment, for a beneficiary's occupation, or for any other reason, and a provision to this effect is contained in cl 8 of the Draft Trustee Bill (1999).

The court's jurisdiction to widen the trustees' investment powers

Trustees who propose to make investments not authorised by the trust instrument or by statute must seek the court's approval.

Initially, such approval would not be given even if it would benefit the trust except in cases of emergency: see *Re Tollemache* (1903). The enactment of s 57 of the TA 1925 and the VTA 1958 afforded the courts greater scope to enlarge the powers of investment.

However, in the 1960s with the enactment of the TIA, the principle was established in cases like *Re Kolb* (1962) and *Re Cooper's Settlement* (1962) that an application for wider investment powers would not be approved save in exceptional circumstances.

By the 1980s, a less sanguine attitude to the TIA had become noticeable. This was exemplified by the Law Reform Committee's Report on Powers and Duties of Trustees (1982) which castigated the Act as 'cumbersome, expensive and outdated'.

The two main criticisms which have been repeatedly levelled against the Act are that:

- the range of investments it permits are unduly restrictive and do not reflect prevailing economic circumstances or take cognisance of various modern investment products;

- the requirement of apportionment which dictates that at least $1/2$ (now $1/4$) of the trust fund must be devoted to narrower range investments is difficult to sustain since equities which are wider range investments have consistently outperformed the various narrower range investments for many years.

As the deficiencies of the TIA became increasingly manifest, the courts began to display a much greater willingness to enlarge the investment powers of trustees in more recent cases such as *Mason v Farbrother* (1983); *Trustees of the British Museum v AG* (1984); *Anker-Petersen v Anker-Petersen* (1991); and *Steel v Wellcome Custodian Trustees* (1988). In the *British Museum* case, in particular, it was held that it is no longer the rule that special circumstances must exist before such an enlargement can be approved.

It is noteworthy that the necessity of seeking judicial approval for the enlargement of trustees' investment powers has now been obviated in the case of pension fund trustees by s 34(1) of the Pensions Act 1995 which provides that the trustees of a pension scheme 'have the same power to make an investment of any kind as if they are absolutely entitled to the assets of the scheme'.

Another significant development was the emergence in 1996 of a Consultation Paper on Trustees' Powers of Investment produced jointly by the Treasury and the Trust Law Committee. This recommended that the current practice of confining trustees to a statutorily prescribed list should be discarded. It proposed in its place a scheme akin to that in the Pensions Act, under which all trustees would, subject to certain safeguards, be empowered to invest trust funds as if they were absolute owners.

Instead of using these recommendations as a platform for proposing new legislation which would completely overhaul the investment regime in the TIA, the Treasury took the less radical step of seeking to amend specific aspects of the Act. This was done by means of an order made pursuant to the Deregulation and Contracting Out Order 1994. The main features of this Order were that:

- it dispensed with the need to apportion trust funds into narrower and wider range parts;

- it removed certain restrictions which were hitherto attached to investing in equities;

- it anticipated the introduction of a new list of authorised investments which would be more comprehensive and up to date than the TIA's authorised investments.

This Order, however, fell with the dissolution of the last Parliament and has not been re-introduced so that the TIA remains in force. It is, however, noteworthy that the Law Commission's Report on Powers and Duties of Trustees echoed earlier criticisms of the TIA and recommended that:

(a) primary legislation should be enacted with a view to reforming the law governing the investment powers of the trustees;

(b) the TIA should be repealed insofar as it is practicable to do so; and

(c) subject to any contrary intention in the trust instrument, the trustee should have the same power to make investments of any kind as if they are absolutely or beneficially entitled to the trust assets.

These recommendations have been incorporated into cl 3 and Sched 2 of the Draft Trustee Bill 1999.

Other duties of the trustee

(a) *Duty to distribute*: Trustees must distribute trust property according to the settlor's wishes. Depending on the circumstances, this may entail the payment of income or the transfer of the trust assets or part thereof to the rightful beneficiaries.

Trustees who make a distribution in favour of a person who is not the rightful beneficiary may be liable for breach of trust: see, for example, *Eaves v Hickson* (1861); and *Re Diplock* (1948).

The trustees may, however, safeguard themselves against liability for wrongful distribution:

- by preliminary inquiries and advertisements under s 27 of the TA for prospective beneficiaries to come forward: see *Re Aldhous* (1955);

- by obtaining *Benjamin orders* in cases where the entitlement of a beneficiary is not in doubt but it is uncertain whether he is still alive: see, for example, *Re Benjamin* (1902); and *Re Greens WT* (1985);

- by insuring against the possibility that a beneficiary whose continued existence or whereabouts is in doubt may subsequently emerge: see *Evans v Westcombe* (1999);

- by applying for appropriate directions in cases where the trustees are unable to resolve a particular issue concerning the distribution of the estate (for example, because the trust is ambiguous).

Where the intended beneficiaries cannot be traced or distribution proves to be impossible or impracticable for some other reason, trustees may as a last resort pay the trust fund into court as happened, for instance, in *Re Gillingham Bus DF* (1958).

(b) *Duty to keep accounts and provide information*: As seen from *Pearse v Green* (1819), a trustee must keep proper accounts.

Such accounts must be open to the beneficiaries who may also require general information from the trustees on the affairs of the trust. Discussions and decisions of trustees are often documented in trust diaries, minute books, etc and *O'Rourke v Darbishire* (1920) has held that 'the beneficiary is entitled to see all [such] documents because they are ... in a sense his own'.

This right of access to trust documents has now been qualified by *Re Londonderry's Settlement* (1965) in relation to documents which record the reasons for the exercise of the trustee's discretions.

The trustee's powers

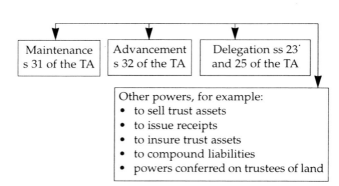

OUTLINE OF TRUSTEE'S MAIN POWERS

Maintenance s 31 of the TA	Advancement s 32 of the TA	Delegation ss 23' and 25 of the TA

Other powers, for example:
- to sell trust assets
- to issue receipts
- to insure trust assets
- to compound liabilities
- powers conferred on trustees of land

The power of maintenance

A trustee cannot obtain a valid receipt for any income paid to an infant beneficiary (IB). He must either retain the income or apply it towards the IB's maintenance, education or benefit under the terms of the trust instrument or by virtue of the power of maintenance in s 31 of the TA. Any income not used to maintain the IB in a given year is accumulated with a view to being invested in authorised securities or carried over and applied towards his future maintenance.

In exercising this power, the trustee is enjoined by s 31 to have regard to:

> ... the age of the infant and his requirements and generally to the circumstances of his case and in particular to what other income is available for the same purpose.

Conditions for exercising the power of maintenance in s 31

(a) The beneficiary must be an infant. Once an IB attains majority, any income accruing from the trust property or his share thereof becomes payable to him unless the trust instrument provides otherwise. In specific terms, this means that:

- If the IB has a vested interest in the property, on attaining majority, he becomes entitled to the capital and any accumulated income not spent on maintaining him during infancy. Alternatively, he may allow the capital to remain in the hands of the trustees who must then pay him whatever income it yields.

- If the IB's interest remains contingent on attaining majority, he cannot demand the capital or any income accumulated during his infancy until the contingency occurs. However, on attaining majority, he becomes entitled to whatever income accrues thereafter from the combined capital and accumulated income in the trustee's hands.

(b) The trust property from which the income is derived (or a part thereof) must be held on trust for the IB in whose favour the power is exercised.

(c) The trustee must not be deprived of the power of maintenance by a contrary intention in the trust instrument; for example:

- a direction to pay the income to someone other than IB; or

- a direction to accumulate the income.

See *Re Ransome* (1957); *IRC v Bernstein* (1961); and *Re McGeorge* (1963).

(d) The nature of the IB's interest must be such that he is entitled to the *intermediate income* accruing during infancy. The position in this regard may be summarised in the opposite diagram.

Payment of income to IB's parents for his maintenance: Instead of applying income generated by the trust property in maintaining an IB, the trustees may pay it to IB's parents or guardians for this purpose. Where they do so, they must ensure that it is properly applied by the parents/guardians: see *Wilson v Turner* (1883).

Maintenance by court order: In addition to the trustee's power under s 31 to maintain an IB out of income, s 53 empowers the court to order the sale of trust property to which the IB is entitled with a view to applying the capital for his maintenance.

Moreover, where the power of maintenance in s 31 is excluded by the terms of the trust, the court may order the trust to be varied in order to allow maintenance: see *Re Collins* (1886).

Nature of interest	Does it carry the intermediate income?
1 Vested interest	Yes: unless settlor intends otherwise
2 Contingent interest under *inter vivos* trust	Yes: unless settlor intends otherwise
3 Contingent interest under testamentary trust: (i) specific bequest/devise (ii) residuary bequest/devise (iii) pecuniary legacy	Yes Yes Only in the following events: • testator is parent or *in loco parentis* to IB and will makes no other provision for IB; • will reveals intention that legacy is to be used to maintain IB; • will directs that legacy is to be set apart from testator's estate
4 Deferred/future interest under testamentary trust: (i) Specific bequest/devise (ii) Residuary bequest of personalty (iii) Residuary devise of realty (iv) Pecuniary legacy	 Yes No, if postponed to a future date (*Re McGeorge*) Arguably carries intermediate income by virtue of s 175 of the LPA Only in situations outlined in 3(iii), above

The power of advancement

What is advancement? According to Viscount Radcliffe in *Pilkington v IRC* (1964), advancement 'means any use of money that will improve the material situation of the beneficiary'. Broadly speaking, advancement entails making provision out of trust capital towards establishing a beneficiary in life before he becomes entitled to demand such capital. For example:

- buying the beneficiary an Army commission: see *Lawrie v Bankes* (1857);

- buying a house for doctor-beneficiary: see *Re Williams WT* (1953);

- paying off beneficiary's debts: see *Lowther v Bentinck* (1874);

- assisting the beneficiary to emigrate: see *Re Long's Settlement* (1868); or start a career at the Bar: *Roper-Curzon v Roper-Curzon* (1871); or set up in business: *Re Kershaw* (1868);

- paying medical and nursing home expenses of the elderly and infirm beneficiary out of capital: see *Stevenson v Wishart* (1987);

- redistributing trust capital under a resettlement which confers tax savings on the beneficiary: see *Pilkington v IRC*.

The statutory power of advancement (s 32): An express power of advancement may be given to trustees in the trust instrument. If not, they may avail themselves of the statutory power in s 32 of the TA unless there is a contrary intention in the trust instrument.

Under s 32, the power of advancement is exercisable in favour of a beneficiary with an interest in trust capital, whether this is:

- an absolute vested interest. In this connection, the power of advancement is typically exercisable where a beneficiary is precluded from claiming the capital as of right because he is an infant or because another beneficiary has a prior right to the income;

- a vested interest which is liable to be defeated (for example, by the exercise of a power of appointment);

- a contingent interest; or

- an interest which is subject to a gift over if the beneficiary dies under a specified age or some other event occurs.

Section 32 contemplates that any capital money advanced may be applied by the trustees themselves or paid to the beneficiary. Where the money is paid to the beneficiary, the trustees cannot stand back and leave it open to him to spend the money as he chooses but must seek to ensure that he applies it to the designated purpose: see *Re Pauling's ST* (1963).

Conditions for exercising the power of advancement in s 32:

(a) The sum advanced must not exceed one half of the vested or presumptive share or interest of the beneficiary in the property. The effect of this can be seen in the following illustrations:

   (i) assuming that T holds £10,000 on trust for B if he attains the age of 21, T may advance up to £5,000 to B;

(ii) if it happens that T holds £10,000 on trust for B1 and B2, who are both infants, in equal shares, each may be advanced up to £2,500;

(iii) it might happen that T holds £12,000 on trust to be divided among all X's sons who are called to the Bar by the age of 30 and X dies leaving four sons under 30, T may advance £1,500 to each son;

(iv) a situation might arise in which B receives one half of his presumptive share and thereafter the half still held by T rises appreciably in value. For example, B's presumptive share may be valued at £100,000 out of which he is advanced £50,000 in 1996. The £50,000 left in T's hand may become worth £70,000 in 1999, thus increasing the total value of B's entitlement to £120,000. *Abergavenny v Ram* (1982) establishes that B cannot receive an additional advancement of £10,000 to reflect the fact that half of his presumptive share is now £60,000, since T is deemed to have exhausted his power of advancement in 1996.

By contrast, if B was advanced £48,000 out of his presumptive share of £100,000 in 1996, this does not exhaust T's power of advancement so that if the £52,000 in T's hands appreciates in value to £72,000, thus increasing B's entitlement to £120,000, T can advance B a further £12,000.

(b) Where B becomes entitled to receive his share of trust property after an advancement has been made in his favour, the sum advanced will be taken into account as part of his share.

(c) The power will not be exercisable to the prejudice of any person entitled to a prior life or other interest, unless such person is of full age and consents in writing to the advancement (as happened for instance in *Pilkington v IRC*).

Note that, if this prior interest arises under a protective trust, and the principal beneficiary gives his consent to the exercise of the power of appointment, this will not operate to determine his interest under the protective trust.

Advancement by court order: The courts have established in cases like *Barlow v Grant* (1684) and *Re Mary England* (1830) that they have an inherent jurisdiction to order payments by way of advancement or maintenance out of the trust capital.

The power of delegation

Traditionally, trustees were considered to be under an obligation to perform their functions personally and not to delegate these functions unless this was provided for by the trust instrument. The operative principle in this regard was *delegatus non potest delegare*: see, for example, *Turner v Corney* (1841).

Where the trust instrument was silent, the courts recognised that delegation could take place within certain well defined limits:

- first, delegation was permitted only where this was justified by legal necessity or ordinary business practice: see *ex p Belcher* (1754); and *Speight v Gaunt* (1883);

- secondly, the trustee could only delegate his ministerial duties and not his discretions: see *Fry v Tapson* (1884);

- thirdly, the trustee was required to take reasonable care not only to appoint a competent agent but also to supervise him properly: see *Matthew v Brise* (1845); *Rowland v Witherden* (1851); and *Fry v Tapson*.

The scope for delegation by trustees has now widened considerably by a number of statutory provisions, most notably:

(a) *Section 23(1) of the TA*: this empowers a trustee instead of acting personally to appoint a solicitor, banker, stockbroker or other agent to transact any business or do any act required to be done in the execution of the trust. It further provides that the appointing trustee shall not be liable for the agent's defaults if he was employed in good faith.

According to Maugham J in *Re Vickery* (1931), the position of the law on delegation by trustees has been revolutionised by s 23(1) which appears to have relaxed the pre-existing rules in two highly significant respects, namely:

- in the first place, Maugham J signified that legal necessity/normal business practice had been dispensed with as a requirement for delegation under s 23(1);

- secondly, he appeared to accept that under s 23(1) a less rigorous standard of care was demanded of the delegating trustee than under the pre-existing law. He derived this conclusion from a combined reading of s 23(1) and s 30(1) of the TA. The former stipulates that a trustee shall not be responsible for the defaults of an agent employed in good faith and the latter that a trustee shall not be liable for acts/neglects/ defaults of a co-trustee or agent unless the same happened through his wilful default. He construed wilful default to mean conscious breach of trust or recklessness.

The manner of Maugham J's juxtaposition of ss 23(1) and 30(1) creates the impression that a trustee who appoints an agent in good faith will not be liable for defaults occasioned by his failure to supervise the agent properly where such failure was neither intentional or reckless. This has been criticised by commentators such as Jones and Martin who insist that it would afford an indolent but well meaning trustee a degree of immunity which he scarcely deserves.

Despite the force of these criticisms, *Re Vickery* cannot be peremptorily dismissed since Maugham, J's view of the import of s 30(1) (though not s 23(1)) has been endorsed by Millett LJ in *Armitage v Nurse* (1927).

(b) *Section 23(2) of the TA*: this empowers a trustee to appoint an agent for the purpose of administering any part of the trust estate situated outside the UK or executing or exercising any discretion or power vested in them in relation to such property. This provision goes beyond s 23(1) in that it empowers trustees to delegate not only the performance of ministerial acts but also any fiduciary discretions exercisable by them.

Note, also, the proposal in the Law Commission's Report on Trustees' Duties and Powers that trustees acting collectively should be able to delegate all their functions (including powers/discretions) apart from their powers to appoint trustees or make decisions regarding distribution of trust assets. Such collective delegation is provided for in cl 11 of the Draft Trustee Bill 1999.

(c) *Delegation of trustee's functions by means of powers of attorney*: s 25 of the TA authorises a trustee to delegate the exercise of all or any of his functions (that is, duties/powers/ discretions). To this end, he must execute a power of attorney and must also give written notice to his co-trustees and any person empowered to appoint new trustees.

Various conditions were inserted into s 25 to prevent excessive delegation by trustees. In particular:

- a trustee would only be allowed to delegate his functions for up to 12 months at a time;

- a trustee could only delegate under the original s 25 if he was leaving the UK for up to one month. This restriction has now been removed by the Powers of Attorney Act 1971;

- under the original s 25, delegation by one trustee to a co-trustee was not permitted where there were no other trustees. Section 25 has now been amended in several respects by the Trustee Delegation Act 1999. One such amendment enables delegation to a sole co-trustee;

- s 25(3) stipulated that the power of attorney had to be signed by the donor and attested by at least one witness. This requirement is now covered by s 1(3) of the Law of Property (Miscellaneous Provisions) Act 1989 and s 25(3) has accordingly been omitted from the amended version of s 25 contained in the 1999 Act;

- s 25 provides that the trustee would remain liable for the acts and defaults of the agent as if they were his own.

Reference must also be made to the Enduring Powers of Attorney Act (EPAA) 1985. This Act seeks to ensure that, if a donor becomes incapable after executing a power of attorney, this will not terminate the power. It was stipulated in s 2(8) of the EPAA that a power of attorney granted under s 25 of the TA could not be an enduring power. At the same time, s 3(3) of the EPAA provided that the donee of an enduring power could execute all or any of the trust functions vested in the donor as trustee. The unintended effect of s 3(3) of the EPAA was that a trustee could by means of an enduring power delegate his functions indefinitely without being subject to the stringent conditions in s 25 of the TA. In view of this, s 3(3) has been termed a 'legislative blunder' by Oerton.

This blunder has now been rectified with the recent repeal of s 3(3) by the Trustee Delegation Act 1999. At the same time, the 1999 Act deals with the mischief s 3(3) was originally intended to address, by allowing a trustee to delegate his trust functions without recourse to s 25 of the TA where the act to be done by the donee relates to land and the trustee-donor has a beneficial interest in the land. This would be the case, for instance, where A and B hold Blackacre on trust for themselves as beneficial owners and A wishes to delegate his dispositive functions over the land in case he loses his mental capacity.

With regard to trustees other than those who are beneficially entitled to trust land, the repeal of s 3(3) means that any delegation of their trust functions by power of attorney will be regulated exclusively by s 25 of the TA.

In addition to the foregoing, s 9 of the TLATA empowers trustees of land to delegate their functions in relation to land to any beneficiary who is of full age and entitled in possession. This may be done for any length of time and must be by means of a non-enduring power of attorney.

In the exercise of such delegated functions, the beneficiary will be liable in the same manner as a trustee. For their part, the delegating trustees shall not be liable for beneficiary's defaults unless they failed to take reasonable care in carrying out the delegation (contrast with s 23 of the TA).

Other powers

These include:

- the power to sell trust property: see, for example, s 16 of the TA; s 1(1) of the TIA; ss 1 and 67 of the Settled Land Act; and s 130(1) of the LPA;

- the power to issue receipts: see, for example, s 14(1) of the TA. Where the receipt relates to the sale of land, it must be issued by at least two trustees except in the case of a trust corporation;

- the power to insure trust property: see, for example, s 19 of the TA;

- the power to compound liabilities: see, for example, s 15 of the TA;

- it is also noteworthy that, where a trust of land is concerned, it is expressly provided by s 6 of the TLATA that, for the purpose of exercising their functions, the trustees shall have in relation to the trust land all the powers of an absolute owner.

Variation of trusts

THE SCOPE FOR VARIATION

Court's approval not needed if all beneficiaries are *sui juris* and entitled to entire beneficial interest: *Saunders v Vautier*	Court's approval required in other cases

Variation under court's inherent jurisdiction	Statutory variation most commonly under s 57 of the TA (1925) and s 1 of the VTA (1958)

Trustees must carry out the trust according to the express terms set out in the trust instrument as supplemented by the various implied terms imposed by statute.

If the beneficiaries wish to vary the terms of the trust, they may invoke the rule in *Saunders v Vautier* (1841) which empowers them to end the trust and reconstitute it under whatever new terms they wish provided they are all *sui juris* and hold the entirety of the beneficial interest in the trust property.

Where the rule in *Saunders v Vautier* does not avail the beneficiaries, any proposed variation must be sanctioned by the court either under its inherent jurisdiction or on the strength of powers conferred by various statutes.

Variation under the court's inherent jurisdiction

Over the years, the courts have in the exercise of their inherent jurisdiction sanctioned variations of trusts in a limited number of situations outlined in *Chapman v Chapman* (1954) such as:

- where the trust instrument directed income to be accumulated in favour of an infant beneficiary without providing for his maintenance, the court could order such maintenance: see *Re Collins* (1866);

- where an unexpected emergency posed a serious threat to the trust, the court could enlarge the trustee's administrative powers to deal with it: see *Re Jackson* (1882); *Re New* (1901); and *Re Tollemache* (1903);

- where a dispute arose regarding the entitlement of beneficiaries under the trust, the courts sometimes sanctioned a compromise which ostensibly settled the dispute but in reality was designed to vary the beneficial interests as set out in the trust instrument. Significantly, in *Chapman*, the House of Lords declined to sanction a variation under this heading because it found that there was no genuine dispute to be compromised.

Variations authorised by statute

(a) *Section 57 of the Trustee Act 1925*: Provides that where, in the management or administration of trust property, it becomes expedient to sell, lease, mortgage or otherwise dispose of such property or to undertake any purchase, investment, acquisition, transfer or other transaction but the trustees have no power to do so under the trust instrument or by law, the court may confer the necessary power on them.

The requirement that there had to be an emergency before additional administrative powers could be conferred under the court's inherent jurisdiction has been dispensed with under s 57 of the TA.

The section has been invoked to confer additional powers on trustees in various contexts, for example:

Case	Nature of power conferred
• *Mason v Farbrother; Anker-Petersen v Anker-Petersen*	To widen existing power to invest
• *Re Power* (1947)	To purchase a home for beneficiaries
• *Re Beale* (1932)	To enable sale of trust land
• *Re Hope* (1929)	To enable sale of settled chattels
• *Re Cockerell's ST* (1956)	To enable sale of residuary estate

It must, however, be noted that s 57 applies only where a proposed variation is intended to enlarge the administrative or managerial functions of the trustees and not where it is intended to redefine or refashion the beneficial interests created by the trust: see *Re Downshire's Settled Estates* (1953).

(b) *The Variation of Trusts Act (VTA) 1958*: Was enacted in response to the House of Lords' refusal to exercise its compromise jurisdiction and approve the proposed variation in *Chapman*. The VTA empowers the court to not only to enlarge the trustee's powers to administer trust property but also to approve arrangements varying or revoking all or any of the terms of the trust (including those relating to the interests of beneficiaries). As Lord Evershed

MR declared in *Re Steed's WT* (1960), the Act has given the judges 'a very wide and indeed revolutionary discretion', in that it now enables them to sanction variations to the terms of a trust in instances where they would previously have felt unable to do so either on the basis of their inherent jurisdiction or under s 57 of the TA.

The four categories

Under the VTA, the court may approve proposed variations on behalf of four categories of persons namely:

(a) Any person who is *unborn*, for example, a trust in favour of A for life remainder to A's eldest son where A as yet has no son. But, *note Re Pettifor's WT* (1966) which indicates that where there is little possibility of any such person being born (for example, a trust in favour of F for life, remainder to her children where F is 70 and childless) the trustee may deal with the trust property on the footing that F will bear no child in future instead of seeking judicial approval for a variation under the VTA.

(b) Any person who is an *infant* or who is *incapable of assenting to the variation because of some other incapacity*: see for example, *Re Whittall* (1973) and *Re CL* (1969).

(c) Any person who has a *discretionary interest under a protective trust*, provided the interest of the principal beneficiary has not been determined.

(d) Any person (whether ascertained or not) who may become entitled to an interest as being at a future date or on the occurrence of a future event a person of a specified description or a member of a designated class. For example:

- where property is held on trust for A, remainder to his wife, and A is a bachelor, the court may approve a variation on behalf of any future wife he may marry: see *Re Clitheroe* (1959);

- where property is held on trust for A for life, remainder to his next-of-kin and A is still alive, the court may approve a variation on behalf of the next of kin: see *Re Moncrieff's ST* (1962).

Note, however, with regard to this fourth category, that the court cannot approve a variation on behalf of any person who would fit the description or would be a member of the designated class if the date had arrived or the event had occurred on the day the application was made to the court. For example, if property is held on trust for A for life remainder to his next-of-kin and A's cousin, C, is the person who would qualify as A's next-of-kin if A was dead on the day the application to vary the trust was made, C must consent to the variation and the court cannot do so on his behalf: see *Re Suffert* (1961).

Benefit
Where a proposed variation is presented to the court for approval on behalf of persons in categories (a), (b) and (d) (but not category (c)), it must be established that it is for the benefit of such persons.

Usually, it is sufficient to show that there will be some financial benefit such as tax savings: see, for example, *Re Druce's ST* (1962); *Re Sainsbury's Settlement* (1967); and *Gibbon v Mitchell* (1990).

The courts have, however, made it clear in cases like *Re Weston's Settlement* (1968); *Re Holt's Settlement* (1969); *Re CL* (1969) that benefit in the present context is not confined to financial gain, but may extend moral or social benefit. In *Weston*, for instance, the court refused to approve a proposed variation of the terms of the trust intended to enable the transfer of trust assets from settlements based in England to off-shore settlements in Jersey. While this arrangement would have produced considerable savings in tax, it would have meant that the settlor's children, on whose behalf approval was sought, would have had to move from England to Jersey which in the court's view was not for their overall benefit. Contrast this with *Re Seale's Marriage Settlement* (1961).

The weight to be accorded to the settlor's intention

The courts must not only ensure that the proposed variation is of benefit to those on whose behalf approval is sought but must enquire whether it runs counter to the settlor's intention. As Evershed MR explained in *Re Steed's WT* (1960), the court will 'look at the scheme as a whole and when it does so consider, as surely it must, what really was the intention of the benefactor'.

However, the Court of Appeal has since decided in *Goulding v James* (1997) that the settlor's intention is material only in determining whether a proposed variation is of benefit to the beneficiaries on whose behalf *judicial* approval is sought. If the variation is undoubtedly beneficial to them, the court will not oppose it simply because it does not reflect the settlor's intention.

Position where adult beneficiary has not consented to variation

The general scheme of the VTA is to secure the consent of all the beneficiaries to the proposed variation with those who are ascertained and who possess the requisite capacity consenting for themselves and the court doing likewise for those not in a position to consent for themselves.

Accordingly, where an adult beneficiary (not being one on whose behalf the court can give approval under s 1) has not consented to a proposed variation the court may adjourn proceedings until his consent is obtained. Such consent is necessary even if the beneficiary merely has a contingent interest which has little prospect of vesting (as in *Knocker v Youle* (1986). If the court mistakenly approves a variation without the requisite consent, it appears from *IRC v Holmden* (1968) that the non-consenting beneficiary is not bound by it and may seek an injunction to prevent the trustees from departing from the original terms of the trust.

6 Remedies for breach of trust

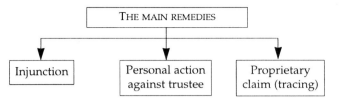

THE MAIN REMEDIES

- Injunction
- Personal action against trustee
- Proprietary claim (tracing)

A breach of trust occurs where a trustee fails to perform any of his duties or improperly exercises any of his powers. The beneficiaries may proceed against a trustee who commits a breach even where the trustee believed that what he was doing was in the best interest of the trust: see *Re Brogden* (1888); unless his act or omission constitutes a mere technical breach which the court would have authorised if leave been sought: see *Lee v Brown* (1798); and *Brown v Smith* (1878).

Injunction

This remedy is available to prevent anticipated breaches, for example:

Case	Purpose of injunction
• *Dance v Goldingham* (1873)	To restrain unauthorised sale
• *Riggal v Foster* (1853)	To restrain unnecessary mortgage
• *Fox v Fox* (1870)	To prevent improper distribution

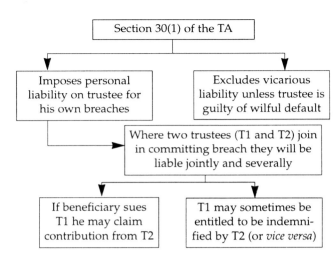

```
┌─────────────────────────────────────┐
│        Section 30(1) of the TA        │
└─────────────────────────────────────┘
        │                      │
        ▼                      ▼
┌──────────────────┐   ┌──────────────────┐
│ Imposes personal │   │ Excludes vicarious│
│ liability on     │   │ liability unless  │
│ trustee for      │   │ trustee is guilty │
│ his own breaches │   │ of wilful default │
└──────────────────┘   └──────────────────┘
        │
        ▼
┌─────────────────────────────────────┐
│ Where two trustees (T1 and T2) join  │
│ in committing breach they will be    │
│ liable jointly and severally         │
└─────────────────────────────────────┘
        │                      │
        ▼                      ▼
┌──────────────────┐   ┌──────────────────┐
│ If beneficiary    │   │ T1 may sometimes  │
│ sues T1 he may    │   │ be entitled to be │
│ claim contribution│   │ indemnified by T2 │
│ from T2           │   │ (or vice versa)   │
└──────────────────┘   └──────────────────┘
```

The personal remedy

Where a breach has in fact been committed by a trustee, s 30(1) of the TA contemplates that he will be personally liable to the beneficiaries for any benefit which he receives as a result as well as any loss suffered by the trust.

A trustee will not, however, be vicariously liable for the breaches of co-trustees or the dishonesty or neglect of agents who act for the trust, unless there has been wilful default on his part as happened, for instance, in *Townley v Sherborne* (1634) where a trustee was affixed with liability for allowing rents collected on trust property to remain in the hands of his co-trustee who misapplied the money. More recently, in *Segbedzi v Segbedzi* (1999), a trustee who by his own neglect allowed his fellow trustees to sell the principal asset of the trust at an undervalue was held liable even though he did not participate actively in the breach.

Liability of incoming and retired trustees

As a rule, an incoming trustee is not liable for breaches committed by his predecessors but, if he becomes aware of such a breach after assuming office, he must take steps to remedy it: see *Re Strahan* (1856).

A retired trustee will, for his part, be liable for breaches he committed while in office but not for breaches committed by other trustees after his departure, unless his retirement was intended to pave the way for the commission of the breach in question: see *Head v Gould* (1898).

Joint liability

Where two or more trustees are involved in committing a breach, their liability is *joint and several* and the beneficiaries may sue all or any of them.

If any one trustee is sued, he may claim a *contribution* from any other trustee who is also liable. Originally, equity required each trustee to make an equal contribution but under the Civil Liability (Contribution) Act 1978, the courts are now able to set the level of each trustee's contribution to reflect the extent of his responsibility for the breach.

Where two trustees are jointly liable for a breach, one may be able to claim an *indemnity* from the other. In particular:

- An indemnity may be claimed against a solicitor-trustee by his co-trustee who has placed complete reliance on the solicitor in the affairs of the trust (see *Chillingworth v Chambers* (1896); and *Re Linsley* (1904)) but not by a co-trustee who, acting on his own judgment, has actively participated: see *Head v Gould* (1898).

- An indemnity may also be claimed by a trustee against his co-trustee where the latter has acted fraudulently in initiating the breach (see *Re Smith* (1896)) but not where the trustee claiming the indemnity has simply abdicated his responsibilities and the breach is occasioned by the honest but erroneous actions of his co-trustee: see *Bahin v Hughes* (1886).

The measure of a trustee's liability

Once a breach of trust is established it becomes necessary to determine the extent of the trustee's liability. This is usually done by reference to the profit which he made or the loss occasioned to the trust estate by the breach. In *Target Holdings v Redferns* (1994), the Court of Appeal went as far as to hold that the obligation to make good the loss arising from a breach remained even if that loss would have been incurred without the breach. This was, however, rejected on appeal by the House of Lords which held that a trustee's liability to make good a breach was fault based. As such, the solicitor-trustee in this case would be liable only if the loss would not have been incurred had it not been for the breach.

The courts have been called upon to determine the liability of trustees in a variety of contexts and the following rules have emerged from their judicial pronouncements:

(a) A trustee who makes an unauthorised investment is liable to pay the difference between the cost of the investment and the price at which it is sold: see *Knott v Cottee* (1852).

If all the beneficiaries are of full age, it has been accepted in cases like *Wright v Morgan* (1926) that they may choose, instead, to adopt the investment. If they do so, but its value has fallen below the price the trustees paid for it, some cases (for example, *Thornton v Stokill* (1855)) suggest that they cannot recover the difference; whereas other cases (for example, *Re Lake* (1903)) suggest they can.

(b) A trustee who improperly retains an unauthorised investment will be liable to pay the difference between the price at which it is sold (or its value at the judgment date if not sold) and what it would have fetched if it had been sold at the appropriate time: see *Fry v Fry* (1859).

(c) A trustee who improperly sells an authorised investment may either be required to replace it or pay the difference between the price at which it was sold and what it will cost to replace it: see *Re Bell's Indenture* (1980).

(d) If a trustee, having improperly sold an authorised investment, invests the proceeds in an unauthorised security and later sells this security for no less than it was bought, he will still be liable for the difference between this amount and the prevailing value of the authorised investment originally held by him. In *Re Massingberd's ST* (1890), it was held that the value of the authorised investment should be determined by reference to the replacement cost at the date the writ was issued; while, in *Re Bell's Indenture,* it was suggested that it should be the replacement cost at the judgment date. In *Jaffray v Marshall* (1994), the court after reviewing both cases signified that it should be the highest intermediate value of the asset between the date of the breach and the judgment date.

(e) Trustees must invest trust funds without undue delay. In the case of a trustee who is merely under a general duty to invest, any undue delay in investing simply renders him liable to pay interest on the uninvested fund. See *Shepherd v Mouls* (1845).

The position is different where the trustee is required by the trust instrument to invest in one type of asset but delays unduly and the cost of the asset increases in the meantime. Cases like *Byrchall v Bradford* (1822) and *Pride v Fooks* (1840) suggest that he will be liable for the difference between what it would have cost to invest at the appropriate time and the increased value of the asset. It has, however, been held in *Robinson v Robinson* (1851) that, where the trustee is given a choice between two investments and delays unduly in selecting one, it is the value of the investment which has performed less favourably that will be used in determining the trustee's liability. This proposition has not found favour with Dillon LJ who argues in *Nestlé v National Westminster Bank* (1993) that, in such an event, the trustees ought to pay a 'fair compensation' for failing to follow a proper investment policy.

(f) Trustees cannot ordinarily set off a profit made from one transaction against a loss from another transaction entered into in breach of trust (see *Dimes v Scott* (1828) and *Wills v Gresham* (1854)) except where the profit and loss resulted from the same transaction or the same policy decision to pursue a particular course of investment: see *Bartlett v Barclays Bank (No 1)* (1980).

(g) Once the extent of the trustee's liability is determined, interest will usually be charged on the sum due from the date of the breach. For a long time, the rate of interest was set at 4% (or 5% in the case of a fraudulent breach) but, nowadays, interest is usually awarded in line with prevailing commercial rates: see, for example, *Wallersteiner v Moir (No 2)* (1975); *Belmont Finance v Williams Furniture (No 2)* (1980); and *Guardian Ocean Cargoes v Banco do Brasil (No 3)* (1994).

Defences to an action for personal liability

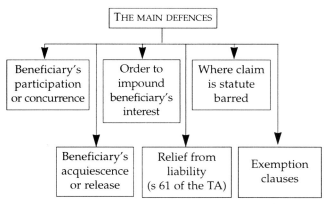

(1) The beneficiary's participation or concurrence in a breach

A trustee has a defence against a beneficiary who participates in or consents to a breach even if the latter derived no benefit. To rely on this defence, the trustee must show that the beneficiary acted of his own free will and understood what he was doing: see *Re Pauling's WT* (1963); and *Holder v Holder* (1968).

This defence cannot be raised against any beneficiary apart from the one who participated/concurred in the breach: see *Fletcher v Collis* (1905).

(2) Acquiescence or release by beneficiary

A trustee will also have a good defence against a beneficiary who learns of a breach after its commission and then releases the trustee from liability or otherwise acquiesces in the breach: see *Walker v Symonds* (1818); *Farrant v Blanchford* (1863); and *Re Garnett* (1885).

(3) Impounding the beneficiary's interest

Where a breach is committed at the instigation or with the consent of a beneficiary, the court may order that his interest should be impounded and applied towards repairing the breach either under its inherent jurisdiction or under s 62 of the TA.

Inherent jurisdiction:

- where a breach is requested/instigated by the beneficiary, his interest can be impounded whether or not he benefited from it: see *Trafford v Boehm* (1746); *Fuller v Knight* (1843); and *Chillingworth v Chambers* (1896);

- where the beneficiary merely consented, his interest will be impounded only where he benefited from the breach: see *Booth v Booth*; and *Chillingworth v Chambers*;

Section 62 of the TA: Authorises a beneficiary's interest to be impounded in the event of a breach whether he benefited from it or not:

- where the beneficiary instigated the breach; or

- where he consented *in writing* to the commission of the breach.

Note, however, that a beneficiary's interest will not be impounded if he asks the trustees to perform an act which is not in itself a breach but the act is carried out by them in a manner which gives rise to a breach: see *Re Somerset* (1894).

(4) Relief from liability under s 61 of the TA

Such relief is available at the court's discretion where a trustee has committed a breach but in so doing has acted honestly and reasonably such that it would be fair to excuse him from liability.

As explained by Byrne J in *Re Turner* (1897), the courts have not sought to lay down strict rules for deciding whether to grant relief but are guided by the circumstances of each case.

Cases in which the courts were prepared to grant relief include:

- *Perrins v Bellamy* (1899): where trustees sold leaseholds belonging to the trust on the erroneous advice of their solicitors;

- *Re De Clifford* (1900): where trust money entrusted by trustees to a solicitor in good faith to defray trust expenses was lost on the solicitor's bankruptcy; and

- *Evans v Westcombe* (1999): where a personal representative had, on legal advice, taken out an insurance policy in favour of a missing beneficiary who later reappeared and brought a claim for an account and lost interest in respect of his share of the estate.

By contrast, cases in which such relief was refused include:

- *Re Turner:* where an ordinary trustee left the affairs of the trust to his co-trustee, a solicitor, who invested in mines which turned out to be worthless; and

- *Re Barker* (1898): where a trustee, on the advise of a commission agent, improperly retained unauthorised investments for 14 years.

(5) Exemption clauses in trust instruments

Exemption clauses are express provisions in a trust instrument which exonerate trustees from acts/omissions that would otherwise constitute breaches of trust. They afford a trustee a good defence whenever he is sued in respect of any breach which comes within the ambit of the clause. They are usually framed in very wide terms as typified by cl 15 of the trust instrument in the leading case of *Armitage v Nurse* which stated that 'No trustees shall be liable for any loss or damage which may happen to the trust fund ... at any time or from any cause whatsoever unless such loss shall be caused by his own *actual fraud*'.

The extent of the immunity given by such widely framed exemption clauses has been a source of contention among academic commentators and has also preoccupied the courts in recent cases.

One matter on which there is more or less universal agreement is that, however widely framed an exemption clause, it cannot exclude a trustee's liability for a breach involving *fraud* or *dishonesty*. The reason for this, as explained by Hayton in his essay on 'The irreducible core content of trusteeship' (and affirmed by Millett LJ in *Armitage*) is that the trustee's duty to act in good faith is a core obligation which is fundamental to the trust and this duty cannot be excluded by a clause which purports to exempt the trustee from liability for dishonesty/fraud.

A further issue which has arisen is whether a trustee can rely on an exemption clause where a breach of trust is caused by his negligence. There is a broad consensus in academic circles that exempting liability for negligence is undesirable, especially where the exemption is being invoked by a professional trustee who has been retained and is being remunerated for his expertise and whose acts and omissions would otherwise constitute professional negligence.

Despite such legitimate concerns, the prevailing judicial position is that, where an exemption clause is framed in such wide terms as that in *Armitage*, it is capable of exonerating a trustee from liability for his breaches of trust even where he is guilty of *gross negligence*. As Millett LJ put it in this case, such a trustee would not be liable for any loss or damage unless caused by his dishonesty, no matter how indolent, imprudent, lacking in diligence, negligent or wilful he might have been. He maintained that an exclusion clause which had this effect was not repugnant to the concept of a trust, since the trustee's core obligations did not, in his view, include the duties of skill and care, prudence and diligence. The position espoused by Millett LJ has been reaffirmed in *Bogg v Raper* (1998) and *Wight v Olswang* (1999) but this has been tempered by the tendency shown by the court in both cases to construe the relevant exemption clauses as restrictively as the wording would permit against the trustees who sought to rely on them.

The Trust Law Committee is currently examining the law relating to the trustee exemption clauses. It remains to be seen how the vexed issue of liability for professional negligence will be resolved in the Committee's recommendations and any ensuing legislation.

(6) Statute barred claims

Various limitation periods are prescribed by statute for different types of action. Thus, s 21(3) of the Limitation Act 1980 lays down the general rule that an action for breach of trust must be commenced not more than six years from the date on which the cause of action accrued. If the action is commenced outside the six year period, the trustee may claim in his defence that it is statute barred unless the action:

- is for fraud or a fraudulent breach of trust to which the trustee is party or privy; or

- is to recover trust property or its proceeds in the trustee's hands or previously received by him and converted to his use.

The proprietary remedy of tracing

This is available where a personal action will not suffice. Tracing is a right *in rem* which may be pursued not only against a trustee who has committed the breach but also against any person to whom he has transferred trust property or assets in breach of trust.

Tracing is available both under the common law and in equity. In the present context, we are primarily concerned with the latter.

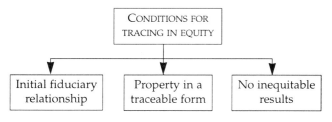

Condition 1
There must be an initial fiduciary relationship
The requirement was recently reaffirmed by Ferris J in *Box v Barclays Bank* (1998) where he declared that:

> ... equitable tracing is only available where there is an equity to trace which requires that there must be an initial fiduciary relationship between the person claiming to trace and the party who is said to have misapplied that person's money.

This requirement is easily satisfied as between trustee and beneficiary not only where their relationship arises under an express trust but also where is arises under a resulting or constructive trust.

Moreover, several cases have affirmed that tracing orders may be made in relation to other types of fiduciary relationships, for example:

Case	Nature of fiduciary relationship
• *Sinclair v Brougham* (1914)	Building society and its depositors: now overruled by the House of Lords in the *Westdeutsche Landesbank* case
• *Re Diplock* (1948)	Executors and deceased's next-of-kin
• *Chase Manhattan Bank v Israel-British Bank* (1981)	Relationship arising from mistaken overpayment by CMB to IBB
• *Boscawen v Bajwa* (1995)	Relationship arising from advance of funds by bank as mortgagor to enable mortgagee to complete purchase of property which ultimately fell through

Condition 2
Property in a traceable form
A tracing order would be futile, unless there is property to trace into. This depends ultimately on what the trustee does with the trust assets in his hands. In this regard, there are various possibilities.

Tracing into unmixed funds

- Where the trust fund remains intact and is kept separately by the trustee (T), the beneficiary (B) is entitled to trace into the fund to the exclusion of T's other creditors.

- Where T withdraws trust money and, without mixing it with his own, uses it to purchase a specific asset, B has a right to trace into the asset. This right entitles B either to claim the asset itself or to treat it as security for the trust money expended on the purchase: see *Re Hallett's Estate* (1880).

- Where T withdraws and squanders trust money without mingling it with his own, B's right to trace in priority to T's other creditors is lost.

Tracing into trust funds which are mixed with trustee's funds

- Where T becomes bankrupt after mixing trust funds with his own, B cannot trace into any part of the mixed fund in priority to T's other creditors, if the mixing was authorised by the terms of the trust: see *Space Investments v Canadian Imperial Bank of Commerce Trust* (1986). If such mixing was done unlawfully, the extent of B's entitlement to trace depends on what thereafter happens to the mixed fund.

- Where no withdrawals are made after mixing, B can lay claim to the part of the mixed fund derived from the trust in priority to T's other creditors: see *Re Hallett*.

- Where T withdraws the mixed fund and purchases specific property with it, it emerges from *Re Hallett*, as well as *Sinclair v Brougham*, that B obtains a first charge over the property purchased to the extent that trust money had been used to purchase it.

If such property later appreciates in value after the purchase, it is unclear whether B can claim a proportionate share of the increased value. It appears from *Hallett* and *Sinclair*, that the charge which arises in B's favour in such circumstances covers only the amount of trust money put into the purchase and does not extend to the increased value of the property purchased. By contrast, other jurisdictions, such as the US and Australia, accept that B will be entitled to a proportionate share of the increased value of property purchased with mixed funds and some support for this approach is found in *Re Tilley's WT* (1967) and *Foskett v McKeown* (1997).

- Where T withdraws part of the mixed fund and squanders it, *Re Hallett* establishes that he is deemed to have spent his own money first, with the result that B will have a prior claim to the balance in the mixed fund in order to recover what is due to the trust.

- Where T after mixing trust funds with his own, purchases property with part of the mixed fund and then squanders the balance, if T is deemed to have spent his own money first (as contemplated by the rule in *Re Hallett*) this would mean in effect that T's money was used to purchase the property while the trust money has been squandered. To avert such an outcome, *Re Oatway* has decided that the rule in *Re Hallett*, does not apply in the present context and affirmed that, in such circumstances, B will have a charge over the property purchased out of the mixed fund in priority to any other creditors of T.

- The position is less clear cut where, after the mixing has occurred, T purchases an asset with part of the mixed fund but retains in the account a balance in excess of or equivalent to the trust money. Assuming the asset has since increased in value, can B lay claim to it? This matter was not specifically dealt with in *Re Oatway* where the whole balance was dissipated after the purchase. A combined reading of *Re Hallett and Re Tilley's WT*, however, suggests that T will be presumed to have spent his own money first so that B's entitlement will be to trace into the balance rather than the asset purchased out of the mixed fund.

• Where T has mixed trust money with his own funds then withdraws part of the mixed fund and later pays in additional money of his own, *Roscoe v Winder* (1915) establishes that B will only be able to trace into the *least intermediate balance* and thus has no priority over T's other creditors in respect of the additional payment. For example, T pays £1,000 of trust money into his account already containing £1,000 of his own money. T then withdraws £1,800, leaving a balance of £200. A week later, T pays £800 of his own money into the account. B can only trace into the £200.

• B's position is even more precarious where the account holding the mixed fund contains a zero balance or is overdrawn at the time of the subsequent payment of T's own money. This may occur for instance where:

(i) T, having paid £1,000 of trust money into his account which already contains £1,000 of his own money, later withdraws the entire £2,000, before paying in £800 of his own money; or

(ii) T's account is overdrawn by £1,500 when he pays in £1,000 of trust money into it and he thereafter pays in £800 of his own money into the same account.

Applying the principle in *Roscoe v Winder*, the intermediate balance in situation (i) would be zero and, in situation (ii), –£500, and so there will be nothing for B to trace into in either instance.

An alternative approach was put forward by Lord Templeman in the *Space Investment* case. Here, a bank-trustee had deposited trust funds in accounts it operated within the bank and was later wound up. Lord Templeman suggested that insofar as these deposits had helped swell the bank's total assets, the beneficiaries ought to be entitled to trace the trust money into all the bank's assets, thus entitling them to a charge over all these assets. This would seem to suggest that, in the two situations referred to above, insofar as T's assets would have been swelled by the injection of £1,000 of trust money, B should be entitled to trace into any asset in the account (that is, the additional £800).

Commentators like Martin, however, insist that such an outcome is supported neither by principle nor by policy and would operate unfairly against T's other creditors. Moreover, although there has been no outright judicial repudiation of Lord Templeman's swollen assets theory, subsequent cases, such as *Bishopsgate Investment Management v Homan* (1994) and *Re Goldcorp* (1995) have sought to minimise its effect by emphasising that:

) Lord Templeman's pronouncement was made *obiter*;

) his Lordship was in fact concerned with tracing into a mixed fund as opposed to a non-existent fund such as an overdrawn account or one with a zero balance.

Both *Goldcorp* and *Homan* affirmed, in accordance with the principle in *Roscoe v Winder*, that, where such a non-existent fund is concerned, the beneficiary loses his right to trace. This has been reinforced by *Re Lewis of Leicester* (1995) and *Box v Barclays Bank*.

- *Backward tracing*: where T borrows money to purchase an asset and thereafter utilises trust funds to pay off the sum borrowed, the question arises as to whether this entitles B to trace into the asset. For example, T obtains an overdraft of £3,000 from his bank which he uses to buy a car. T then pays off the overdraft with £3,000 of trust money (leaving a zero balance). Can B claim priority over T's other creditors by tracing into the car? This issue was considered in *Homan* where there was a marked divergence of judicial opinion.

  On the one hand, Vinelot J and, on appeal, Dillon LJ, recognised the possibility of such 'backward tracing' in certain narrowly defined circumstances, notably:

  ɔ where T acquired an asset with money borrowed from an overdrawn or loan account and there was an inference that the borrowing was done with the intention that it would be repaid with the misappropriated trust funds;

  ɔ where the misappropriated trust funds were paid into T's overdrawn account in order to reduce the overdraft and enable T to draw further sums from the account to purchase the asset.

  On the other hand, Leggatt LJ refused to countenance a tracing claim in respect of an asset acquired before the misappropriation and hence without the aid of trust money.

- *Tracing and subrogation*: Where money is provided by T to discharge a debt owed to C, a secured creditor (for example, a mortgage debt) and the tracing process discloses that this was trust money, it has been established in *Boscawen v Bajwa* that the right of subrogation is available to B. This entitles B to step into C's shoes and assert whatever proprietary right C might have over the asset which secured the debt.

Tracing into two trust funds which have become mixed together

- Where funds from two separate trust funds administered by the same trustee are mixed with his own funds, the rule in *Re Hallett* applies so that he is deemed to have spent his own money first.

- As between the two trust funds whose monies have been mixed, the position is determined primarily by reference to the rule in *Clayton's Case* (1816). Under this rule, the first of the two trust funds to be paid into the account is deemed to have been withdrawn first, so that the beneficiaries under the second trust will be entitled to trace into the balance of the account in priority to the beneficiaries of the first trust. It has, however, been held in *Barlow Clowes v Vaughan* (1992) that this 'first in-first out' rule is no more than a rule of convenience and will not be used to determine such competing claims where the court discovers a contrary intention, whether express or implied.

- Where specific property is purchased with money from the mixed fund, both sets of beneficiaries will have a charge over the property purchased and will rank *pari passu* in proportion to the share of the purchase price derived from their respective trust funds: see *Sinclair v Brougham*.

It has been established in cases like *Re Diplock* that B's right to trace extends to situations where T transfers trust money or property to an innocent volunteer (V).

- Where the trust money remains intact or the trust property remains undisposed of in V's hands, B will have no difficulty in recovering it from him through the process of tracing.

- Where V sells such trust property after receiving it and keeps the proceeds separate from his own funds, B becomes entitled to trace into the proceeds.

- Where the trust money received by V (or the proceeds of the sale of trust property given to him) is mixed with V's own money and withdrawals subsequently made from the mixed fund leaving a balance, the position of V and B, vis à vis this balance, is ordinarily determined by reference to the 'first in-first out rule' in *Clayton's Case*.

- Where property is subsequently purchased using the mixed fund, V and B will rank *pari passu* in their respective entitlements in accordance with the rule in *Sinclair v Brougham*.

Condition 3
No inequitable results

Like all equitable remedies, the remedy of tracing is discretionary and will not be awarded if, in the court's view, to do so would lead to inequitable results: see *Re Diplock*.

Closely allied to the proposition that tracing will be disallowed if it produces inequitable results is the doctrine of change of position. The possible application of this doctrine in the sphere of tracing has been acknowledged by the House of Lords in *Lipkin Gorman v Karpnale* (1991).

The effect of the doctrine in this sphere may well be that where V, acting in good faith, utilises trust money received by him in improving his own property or has committed himself to other expenditure which he would not have done if the trust money had not been available to him, the court can relieve him wholly or in part from his liability to make restitution to B.